The Reminiscences Of
Mr. John B. Vaessen
Pearl Harbor Survivor

Interviewed By
Paul Stillwell

U.S. Naval Institute • Annapolis, Maryland

Copyright © 2012

Preface

This oral history originated with a letter from Mr. Vaessen in 1987. He lived in California and wanted to record his recollections of service on board the target ship *Utah* (AG-16) in the waning days of 1941. His service had indeed been both dramatic and admirable. When the Japanese air raid hit Pearl Harbor in December of that year, the *Utah* capsized. Vaessen realized that the ship was turning over but had no idea why. Even so, he was at his battle station below decks and kept the ship's electrical power supply going as long as he could, thus providing light that enabled shipmates to see their way to safety. Then he rapped on the bottom of the ship until rescuers cut a hole in the overturned hull and freed him. Admiral Chester Nimitz, Commander in Chief Pacific Fleet, awarded Vaessen, then a fireman second class, a Navy Cross for his heroism.

By coincidence, I was due for Naval Reserve active duty training in California soon after Mr. Vaessen's letter arrived. One evening, during a break from the training, I got together with him on Treasure Island in San Francisco Bay. At the time it was still the site of an active naval facility; it has since been shut down. He was energetic in recalling his memories. Indeed, we went back to talk about his youth during the Depression, with the intent of capturing recollections of his entire naval service and using the pre-Navy years as background. When we parted, we hoped to get together for record the rest of his naval service, but that, unfortunately, never happened.

The 1987 interview was transcribed by Deborah Reid, then a member of the Naval Institute staff. For the next quarter century it was stuck in the Naval Institute backlog until I heard from retired Command Master Chief Tom Helvig, who is a selfless volunteer in publishing electronic newsletters concerning the battleships *New Jersey* (BB-62) and *Iowa* (BB-61). A California friend of his, retired Chief Communications Technician Ron Welker, had served with Helvig, and they remained in contact. At Tom Helvig's request, Chief Welker visited Mr. Vaessen for an interview and also secured Mr. Vaessen's signature on the document enabling the Naval Institute to publish the 1987 interview. I have done only slight editing of the original transcript and have added footnotes to provide additional background information. Ms. Janis Jorgensen of the Naval Institute staff has coordinated the printing and binding of the finished product.

In completing this volume, the Naval Institute expresses its gratitude to the Tawani Foundation and the Pritzker Military Library of Chicago for their generous financial support of the oral history program that produced this memoir.

Paul Stillwell
U.S. Naval Institute
June 2012

Deed of Gift

The U.S. Naval Institute is hereby authorized to make available to individuals, libraries, and other repositories of its choosing the tapes and/or transcripts of an oral history interview concerning the life and naval career of the undersigned. The Naval Institute may also, at its discretion, use the material in electronic/digital format, including posting on the Internet. The interview was recorded on 11 June 1987 in collaboration with Paul Stillwell for the U.S. Naval Institute.

The undersigned does hereby release and assign to the U.S. Naval Institute the rights and title to these interviews, with the exception that the undersigned retains the right to use the material for his own purposes, as he sees fit. The copyright in both the oral and transcribed versions shall be the property of the U.S. Naval Institute. The tape recordings of the interviews are and will remain the property of the U.S. Naval Institute.

Signed and sealed this ___28___ day of __APRIL__ 2012.

Original copy is signed, though barely visible

John B. Vaessen

Oral History Interview with Mr. John B. Vaessen
Date: 11 June 1987
Place: U.S. Naval Station, Treasure Island, California

Paul Stillwell: Mr. Vaessen, it's a real pleasure to see you this evening and have an opportunity to get your recollections. Just to get some background, before we get into the Navy part, perhaps you could tell when and where you were born and some of your boyhood memories, please.

John Vaessen: I was born in San Francisco, California, at St. Francis Hospital. Until she died, the woman that was the nurse on the job, my mother and her were great friends. I was about 25 years old when she passed away, so that was a long-lasting friendship there.

Paul Stillwell: When were you born?

John Vaessen: July 10, 1916.

Paul Stillwell: What do you recall about your parents?

John Vaessen: My father died when I was three years old, but he was maitre d' at the Fairmont Hotel.* He had worked at the other hotels. He originally came out here when the St. Francis was either built or remodeled, I don't know which. He and the chef and a baker, because they wanted established people. But then all these people, they move around a lot, so he worked a little bit at the Palace. He didn't care for it. Then he went up to the Fairmont; he liked it the most. So he stayed most of his time there.

---

* The Fairmont Hotel, atop Nob Hill, opened in 1907, a year after the great San Francisco earthquake and fire.

Paul Stillwell: Do you have any memories of it at all?

John Vaessen: Yes, I crapped my pants once, and I remember him carrying me out so my mother could change.

Paul Stillwell: Did your mother ever remarry?

John Vaessen: No, she did not.

Paul Stillwell: So then it fell on her to support the family.

John Vaessen: Yes. I have a younger sister named Virginia. My grandmother was living in Sonoma, so my mother moved up there temporarily, supposedly. She got a job later on as a switchboard operator for the telephone. It was the California Telephone and Light at that time, but these companies keep changing. Eventually, she got to be the night operator, because then she could be at home during the day while we were there or in school. Later on we were in school. So I went to the Sonoma Valley High and Sonoma High School, and I graduated. I did not have any honors or anything like that; I just graduated. I was a student.

Paul Stillwell: What ambitions did you have as a boy?

John Vaessen: Mostly to get a job. In those days you couldn't buy a job.

Paul Stillwell: How did the Depression affect your family?[*] Did your mother work steadily?

---

[*] Following the crash of the New York Stock Exchange in late October 1929, the United States was plunged into the Great Depression, from which it did not recover until the nation geared up for World War II at the beginning of the 1940s. The Depression was marked by high unemployment and many business failures.

John Vaessen: Yes. They had what they called AR—absent on rotation. That was what is now the five-day week. It used to be six days. So every week, which day is it, it used to be different ones. Then they were required to get three subscribers a year to hold onto your job. Of course, Boise Springs is close by, and that was a resort area, so these people, when they close up for the winter, then she'd go back in the spring and sign them up, so it made it a little easier. Some of the people in the other towns didn't find it that easy.

Paul Stillwell: Did you take jobs as a boy to supplement the family income?

John Vaessen: I worked in the theater. I didn't sell tickets; I took the tickets, I handed out the programs, I swept it out. After school, when I was in high school, I worked there helping the janitor, and would come in on Saturdays and clean up the basketball court and the auditorium, put the chairs away, that kind of stuff.

Paul Stillwell: How hard did the Depression hit Sonoma? Were there a lot of people out of work?

John Vaessen: Yes, but they had a lot of pride, and you would never know it. We had some friends that used to love to go fishing about three times a week. Of course, I was young then and didn't realize that the fish was their food.

Paul Stillwell: Did you actually live with your grandmother?

John Vaessen: No, no, never did. She said, "I raised my children, you raise yours."

Paul Stillwell: So was it just you and your sister in the house while your mother was working?

John Vaessen: Yes. But we were in school. And when she got on at nights, this solved a lot of problems, because then she could be home during the day. Even if she was sleeping, she was there.

Paul Stillwell: I would think it would be sort of traumatic for young children to not have a mother there when they're trying to sleep at night.

John Vaessen: Well, you can get used to anything. Like they say, the human body can take all kinds of punishment. The only thing it can't take is prosperity. And that's true.

Paul Stillwell: Did you have any interest or hobbies as a boy?

John Vaessen: Nothing special, always around looking for a job. I caddied at the gold links—that would be on the weekend—and it was three miles away. I walked there and I walked back so I could have enough money to buy a bicycle to get there. This is the way things were. You make do the best you can.

Paul Stillwell: Were you involved with Boy Scouts?

John Vaessen: No, couldn't afford it. It was $12.00 a year.

Paul Stillwell: Were you an athlete in school?

John Vaessen: Not very good, no.

Paul Stillwell: How much did you keep track of the world events? In the '30s, of course, the Japanese were making trouble in the Far East.

John Vaessen: We all kind of knew it, but it didn't bother us. We had Japanese living across the street from us. They raised asparagus and had 40 acres. They were just as good. We had some Japanese in the high school, a German mother and Japanese father. We treated them like anybody else.

Paul Stillwell: Did you read a fair amount as a boy?

John Vaessen: Yes, some. I delivered papers, so I would read the papers, not thoroughly.

Paul Stillwell: Enough to keep informed.

John Vaessen: Yes. I kind of knew what was going on. I remember when Lindbergh landed.* We sold extra papers that day, of course.

Paul Stillwell: I'm sure you did.

John Vaessen: And the great crash, the stock market crash. Of course, I didn't know what it meant; I had no idea.

Paul Stillwell: Did things seem more ominous in the '30s, after the Depression started, than during this prosperity?

John Vaessen: I don't know. I was too young to realize what was going on. I remember all the bootleggers and all that kind of stuff.† I mean, I knew where they were. I knew of them. I mean, what they were doing was fine with me. It was easy. They had these pro-highs that would go out looking for them, but what the

---

* Charles A. Lindbergh became a national hero when he made the first solo flight across the Atlantic Ocean in May 1927. The light cruiser *Memphis* (CL-13) brought Lindbergh and his plane back to the United States, arriving at the Washington Navy Yard on 11 June.
† The 18th Amendment to the Constitution was ratified in 1919 and went into effect in 1920, prohibiting the consumption of alcoholic beverages in the United States. The Volstead Act, enacted by Congress in 1919, spelled out the penalties for violations. In December 1933 the ratification of the 21st Amendment to the Constitution repealed the 18th and thus ended national prohibition.

hell? They all had beehives and the bees would get you, so they couldn't get in to them.

Paul Stillwell: Did the job at the movie theater include the opportunity to see movies free, as well?

John Vaessen: Yes, but you'd see it once or twice. You were busy taking the tickets, getting snatches of it here and there. All the people I knew were coming and going. I amused myself by watching people fumbling, "I'll get the tickets. I'll get 'em." [Laughter] And they were not producing the money, but somebody would come up with it.

Paul Stillwell: How much chance was there for a social life during your school years?

John Vaessen: We had enough. I mean, not as much as most people had.

Paul Stillwell: Recreation was relatively cheap at that point.

John Vaessen: Yes, it was no problems.

Paul Stillwell: How much a part did religion play in the life of the family?

John Vaessen: My mother was Christian Scientist. She got it through my father, because he died when I was three, and he took awful sick. He stopped in at one of the lectures. Of course, he went home and told my mother about it, and then she got interested in it. She kind of followed that pretty strongly. But I had to go to Sunday school. I didn't get that much out of it.

Paul Stillwell: Did you become a Christian Scientist yourself?

John Vaessen: No, no. They've got their points.

Paul Stillwell: When you graduated from high school, what plans did you have at that point in life?

John Vaessen: I was looking for a permanent job. That was everybody's ambition. Anything.

Paul Stillwell: What year was that?

John Vaessen: Nineteen thirty-five. I worked in a cannery for a bit, putting the sugar in the peaches. It would spill all over me, and then I'd go out and eat lunch, and the bees would come around. So I had to stay indoors. [Laughter]

Paul Stillwell: Is this for the Libby Company?

John Vaessen: No, this was Sabastiani Cannery in Sonoma. He was an independent man there. He had a winery there. It was illegal at that time. But he built a cannery and kept the money at home. He had a lot of property. If you've ever been to Sonoma Valley, you can see his name all around there.

Paul Stillwell: Did you have any specific career in mind, or was it going from job to job?

John Vaessen: It was trying to find something steady.

Paul Stillwell: How long did the cannery job last?

John Vaessen: That was just in the summer. Of course, I also worked for other people in their orchards. I picked every kind of fruit you could think of, except oranges, which they don't have in Sonoma Valley. I'd pick prunes, apples, peaches, pears, cut them and dried them, sulfured them.

Paul Stillwell: Did you see the families as they'd come out from the Midwest?

John Vaessen: Yes. Saw a lot of them.[*] At one place where I worked all night, I was on the night shift there peeling apples. They had two girls, they would drop into a bin, and they would cut out the bad parts. Then they were sliced up and then put in a drier. You see them in the stores—dried fruit. That was only in the summer, and the owner of that place let those people stay in their little trailers and tents and whatnot. Most of them worked there.

Paul Stillwell: How long did this period last for you?

John Vaessen: One year. About a year.

Paul Stillwell: What sort of work did you get into after that?

John Vaessen: One day I got a call from a fellow in town. He was an electrician, a contractor, and he needed help. He was doing a job someplace, and would I be interested? So I went up and gave him a hand. He said, "How about coming back tomorrow?" And it kept going. It wasn't every day; it was most days of the week. So that was very interesting, I thought. FHA was just coming into its own then, and there were more houses being built.[†] The economy was getting better.

Paul Stillwell: From what you describe, Sonoma did better than many places in the country at this time.

---

[*] Author John Steinbeck's most famous work was *The Grapes of Wrath*, published in 1939, which told of the oppressive forces facing Oklahoma farmers who sought work in California during the Depression. The book won the 1940 Pulitzer Prize for literature and was made into a popular movie starring Henry Fonda.
[†] FHA – Federal Housing Administration.

John Vaessen: Yes, everybody had their own food. We never had to buy vegetables or fruit, because everybody gave everybody else.

Paul Stillwell: Sort of a barter economy?

John Vaessen: Yes. I mean, people come over here with a bucketful of grapes.

Paul Stillwell: Did you have in mind at that point to be an electrician as a specific trade?

John Vaessen: That kind of interested me. I got my Social Security number. My mother got me in the telephone company. Of course, there I was like a janitor, but I delivered phone books. In those days, you'd deliver a phone book, and you'd pick up the old one so people wouldn't be using it. Then I'd get paid for how many I picked up, not how many I delivered, which I thought was a hell of a good method.

Paul Stillwell: It assured that it got done.

John Vaessen: Made damn sure. Nowadays they just flop them around. So anyway, I did that. Any job that would come up that had money involved, I was there.

Paul Stillwell: Did the electrician work last longer than most?

John Vaessen: Yes, he kept calling me back, "Come on tomorrow. Come the next day," and so forth. I got friendly with him. Then pretty soon, things were picking up, and he hired another fellow. He eventually went over to a competitor, but we're still good friends.

Paul Stillwell: Was this essentially on-the-job training for you?

John Vaessen: Yes. No bookwork. I mean, you do it or you don't do it.

Paul Stillwell: With the steady building, then, you were assured.

John Vaessen: It slowly increased.

Paul Stillwell: How long did that job last for you?

John Vaessen: Off and on, I guess about two years.

Paul Stillwell: When would that have been, 1936 to '38, perhaps?

John Vaessen: I'm not sure of that, because I would do other things in between too.

Paul Stillwell: Did you have any romantic interests at the time?

John Vaessen: Not really.

Paul Stillwell: You continued to live at home, I presume.

John Vaessen: Yes. Yes, I did that for quite a while.

Paul Stillwell: What sort of arrangement did you have? Was this income kicked into the family kitty, and then you drew an allowance?

John Vaessen: First of all was to buy your own clothes, and then later on, you buy your own car. First I bought a bike, and then I bought a car. You take care of that; that was the main thing.

Paul Stillwell: What made the Navy appealing to you when you decided to join up?

John Vaessen: The draft was coming up. At one time, the Army marched through Sonoma, which I thought was one great idea. They had these guys march from town to town, and they brought all their supplies there and they camped in town. It looked like a lot of hardship there. I thought, "Gee, in the Navy you wouldn't be quite that bad."

Paul Stillwell: How much knowledge did you have specifically about the Navy at that point?

John Vaessen: Mare Island was not too far away, and they used to have Navy Day.* In the school, I think they'd run a busload of us down there a couple of times, and that looked pretty interesting.

Paul Stillwell: Did you have any romantic ideas about the Navy? There were newsreels and novels and so forth about it.

John Vaessen: No, I didn't.

Paul Stillwell: Some people have joined because they were seeking a sense of adventure.

John Vaessen: Well, I knew you would be going places.

Paul Stillwell: How did it specifically come about that you enlisted?

---

* Mare Island Navy Yard, Vallejo, California, began operation in September 1854. It was the Navy's first shipyard on the West Coast. The shipyard was decommissioned in April 1996 as the result of the Base Realignment and Closure Process.

John Vaessen: My friend and I—he lived out in Buena Vista.

Paul Stillwell: What was his name?

John Vaessen: Sam Budna. He's deceased now. Cedric Budna, but they called him Sam. He was the second child of the family. We would go out. When we had a car, we would go up to the Russian River, and they had a roller-skating rink up there. We would go roller-skating, and we would do different things. We'd pick up a couple of fellows, did a lot of crazy things. We stopped in Santa Rosa one time, and Naval Reserve was there. So we went in and inquired about it, and thought that wouldn't be too bad, you know, rather than the Army. That looked a little better. So we went in and talked to the guy in charge. His name was—I'm not positive—Gordon Brown. He was a disk jockey in the local radio station, and he was a commander, or whatever you call it. But we found out this was strictly a radio class, and we got to meet the different people there, all nice guys, lived in different parts of Santa Rosa, mostly. So we went to several meetings, and we found it interesting.

Paul Stillwell: Was this before you signed the paper and took the oath?

John Vaessen: I think I had signed first, and then my friend Sam, he says, "You know, I think I'll get in on that too. Gee, the way this draft thing is, that looks the best."

Paul Stillwell: What month and year did that take place that you enlisted?

John Vaessen: I don't know. A couple of years before.

Paul Stillwell: So probably around 1939 or '40?

John Vaessen: Could be, yes. When I was called up, I think I had about two years. That's why I was seaman first class, and then they changed it to fireman later on, second class.

Paul Stillwell: So at what point did you get in uniform?

John Vaessen: Not until you went for active duty.

Paul Stillwell: You went to these meetings how often?

John Vaessen: I think they were once a month. They would discuss different things—life aboard ship, different details that you would have to do, you know, that kind of stuff.

Paul Stillwell: Was there specific training in radio procedures?

John Vaessen: No. The fellows I talked to later kind of laughed, because we used to muster by radio. The guy says, "That's the Navy I want to be in." [Laughter]

Paul Stillwell: What do you mean, muster by radio?

John Vaessen: Who was at the meeting. Just like aboard ship, you know, you come out every morning and they count heads. But there, he would send out a radio signal. I don't know where it went. Who was there.

Paul Stillwell: [inaudible]

John Vaessen: I guess. I don't know. Anyway, the guys were proficient in that. They did that. So and so was here.

Paul Stillwell: What civilian job did you have while you were attending these drills?

John Vaessen: Oh, gee, I don't know, there were so many jobs. [Laughter] It's hard to say.

Paul Stillwell: At what point did you start working for the shipyard?

John Vaessen: That was 1940.

Paul Stillwell: How did that come about?

John Vaessen: I signed up there. Of course, every opening there was, you signed up for it.

Paul Stillwell: Were there waiting lists?

John Vaessen: There were people waiting to be called, yes. So, anyhow, they figured I had enough experience, so I went to the shipyard as electrician's helper, which was fine with me.

Paul Stillwell: This was Mare Island?

John Vaessen: Mare Island Shipyard, yes.

Paul Stillwell: What do you remember about your job there?

John Vaessen: The first day I was on a destroyer, and they were pulling in cable. First of all, I had to go and put light bulbs in so we could see what was going on.

Paul Stillwell: Was this ship just being built?

John Vaessen: No, it was an old four-stacker.* They had Lend-Lease, and these were some.†

Paul Stillwell: Destined for the British.

John Vaessen: No, they were pulled out for the American forces.

Paul Stillwell: They would go out of mothballs, is that it?

John Vaessen: Just previously, you know. They hadn't been out of mothballs that long.

Paul Stillwell: So they needed some work.

John Vaessen: Yes. They needed a lot of work. [Laughter] Anyhow, I was on there and I was assigned to different people. They would have a gang to pull in cables. Sound was just coming in at that time.‡ Of course, that was a lot of modification. There's always changes aboard ship. We would learn how to pack these tubes on watertight bulkheads, strap them to cables, all those kind of things. Little by little, you learned your way around.

Paul Stillwell: What kind of shape was the ship in? Corroded?

John Vaessen: I don't know. Crowded, yes. But I didn't know that much about

---

* The standard U.S. destroyers built during World War I and in the early 1920s had four smokestacks. During the period between World Wars, some were taken out of the active fleet and painted with red-lead preservative. A number of the destroyers were reactivated for World War II.
† The Lend-Lease Act, passed by the U.S. Congress on 11 March 1941, was a device that enabled the United States to provide military aid to Great Britain without intervening directly in the European war then in progress. The program was later expanded to include aid to other Allied nations as well.
‡ This is a reference to sonar equipment.

them myself.

Paul Stillwell: Did you work at that job until you went on active duty?

John Vaessen: Yes. I had worked in a gas station too. I forgot about that. I worked for Standard Station. I left Standard Stations to work at the shipyard.

Paul Stillwell: How long would you guess you worked at the shipyard?

John Vaessen: I went there in November of '40. In May of '41, I was called to active duty. So it was less than a year—about six months.

I'll never forget Lieutenant Boyes, personnel, I guess he was, and he says, "Oh, under the law you're entitled, when you come back, to have one year's work."* I don't know if you remember that or not. You're probably too young for that.

Paul Stillwell: They had that provision later on.

John Vaessen: That was just a new law, so he wanted to make sure that I was aware of that.

Paul Stillwell: Do you remember any other specific experiences from the time you worked at Mare Island? There must have been other ships that you were involved with.

John Vaessen: Yes. It was very fascinating to watch them launch *Fulton*.

---

* Lieutenant Gordon M. Boyes, USN (Ret.), was on active duty at the Mare Island Navy Yard. Many retired naval personnel were recalled to active duty for service as war approached.

John B. Vaessen Interview (6/11/87) – Page 17

Paul Stillwell: Submarine tender.[*]

John Vaessen: Sub tender. That's quite a deal.

Paul Stillwell: I imagine there was a great feeling of patriotism at the time.

John Vaessen: Oh, yes. Of course, all the stories that were flying around there, like *California* was built there, and I don't know if you've heard the story of how it splashed all the mud on the main street in town later on when they launched it.[†]

Paul Stillwell: No.

John Vaessen: I've talked to people that were there. They were old-timers at this time, that had worked on the *California*, and they told me what had happened. It seems there was a young ensign or lieutenant, some naval officer, and he was interested in hydraulics. This was something new. So when they launch a ship, they take chains and coil them up. Then they put a cable around it and bring it onto the ship, all along the side of the ship. Because when it hits the water, it's got an awful drag to it.

Paul Stillwell: They slow down the momentum.

John Vaessen: Yes, they slow down the momentum till the tugs grab hold. So the story was that this officer thought, "We could use hydraulics on this, instead of all these chains," because it took time to coil them all up, tie them up, and everything. So they rigged up a hydraulic system. Everything worked fine until all the hoses popped. The ship came, of course it went sideways, and all the people on the dock

---

[*] The *Fulton* (AS-11) was launched at Mare Island on 27 December 1940 and commissioned 12 September 1941.
[†] The battleship *California* (BB-44) was launched at Mare Island on 20 November 1919 and commissioned 10 August 1921.

in Vallejo were watching, and all this muddy water just splashed all over them.

Paul Stillwell: Were you involved with the union while you were working there at the shipyard?

John Vaessen: No, there was no union there.

Paul Stillwell: I imagine that your knowledge was growing steadily during this period.

John Vaessen: Oh, yes, every day. I learned something every day, even today.

Paul Stillwell: Any other specific ships you recall working on? Were you involved in new construction work?

John Vaessen: Yes, I was. I don't know if that was the *Fulton* or the *Sperry*. It could have been the *Fulton*. I was on there for a bit. They would paint the wire ways, where it was to be, and then I'd go with the welder and clean it up and weld these little buttons so they could strap the cables.

Paul Stillwell: Any particular memorable experiences?

John Vaessen: Yes, I mean, funny things happened.

Paul Stillwell: Such as?

John Vaessen: Do you know what a driller is? He works in shop 11 with the ship fitters, and if you've got a hole to be drilled in the metal, they do it. They were on the *Fulton* or the *Sperry*, one of them, and they had to drill some holes in a bulkhead.* So they drill the holes, and all of a sudden oil comes flying out. There were some barrels of oil on the other side, and it ruptured. [Laughter]

Paul Stillwell: Went right through the side of the barrel?

John Vaessen: It came through a hole. They thought they had drilled into an oil tank. [Laughter]

Paul Stillwell: Which probably wouldn't have been filled at that point.

John Vaessen: No. But these are funny stories.

Paul Stillwell: How did it come about that you went on active duty? Did you volunteer to do that?

John Vaessen: No, they volunteered me.

Paul Stillwell: And that's the point at which you got your uniform?

John Vaessen: No, still didn't get a uniform. I was sworn in at Goat Island.†

Paul Stillwell: Very close to where we are now.

John Vaessen: Yes, right up the hill. Of course, there were funny incidents there. I came back there later.

Paul Stillwell: What are some of the funny incidents you recall from Goat Island?

---

* The submarine tender *Sperry* (AS-12) was launched at Mare Island on 17 December 1941 and commissioned 1 May 1942.
† Goat Island was a nickname for Yerba Buena Island in San Francisco Bay. This interview was conducted at nearby Treasure Island, located between San Francisco and Oakland. It served as the site of a world's fair in 1939-40, then was converted for use as a Navy base during and after World War II.

John Vaessen: Well, my neighbor friend, Sam, had been called in a week or two before, and he was there working on the *Boston*, I think it was.* They were cleaning the thing—makework. So I said, "What are all these PALs I see around here?" I didn't know what they were. They were prisoners-at-large. I had no idea what they were. Then it come time to eat. We still had civilian clothes, because they didn't have uniforms, enough to go around. So come time to eat there, we all lined up, and I see highway patrol, I saw guys with white jackets, I see doctors, everybody eats here. They went in. Everybody was eating on the Navy, I guess. You know, money was scarce.

Paul Stillwell: The Navy didn't have any system for deciding who could eat and who couldn't?

John Vaessen: I don't know. They were all doing something, I guess, to avoid a ticket. There was the highway patrol. I mean, I was amazed at all these people freeloading.

Paul Stillwell: Were you issued some kind of an identification?

John Vaessen: Yes, a civilian pass or something.

Paul Stillwell: Hadn't you, in fact, enlisted, so you would have a Navy ID card?

John Vaessen: We weren't sworn in as yet.

Paul Stillwell: Was this time you had spent with the Naval Reserve sort of an informal arrangement then?

---

* USS *Boston*, a protected cruiser, was commissioned in 1887. From 1918 to 1946 she was at Yerba Buena Island as a receiving ship, that is, a floating barracks. In 1940 she was renamed *Despatch* so the name *Boston* could be used for a new heavy cruiser. The *Despatch* was reclassified as IX-2 in February 1941.

John Vaessen: Yes. I don't know the details.

Paul Stillwell: Had you gotten paid by the Navy at all before then?

John Vaessen: No, no, nothing. They didn't pay us.

Paul Stillwell: It sounds almost like a voluntary thing.

John Vaessen: Yes, you volunteer; that's what you do. You sign your name and if you're called up, you're called up, that's it.

Paul Stillwell: But evidently, even though you hadn't enlisted, that was enough to protect you from the draft, I take it.

John Vaessen: Yes. You knew where you were going to go. Anyway, while we're in the chow line, all of a sudden, here comes a Marine with four PALs coming, and they all come and have priority.* They marched on through, and they got fed first, and they sat at the table. When they get all through, they put all their silverware in a cup, whether they're through eating or not, and away they go. But they weren't pals. [Laughter]

Later on, the second time I was there, when I was putting the *Starling* in commission, I reported up there and was sent down here.† I was on the messenger watch, and here comes a taxicab with a bunch of sailors. That goes on all the time. Here comes this cab driver. He comes up and says, "I want to know where I turn myself in."

I said, "Gee, I don't know." So I got the OD, and he didn't know.‡ Anyhow, I found out that during World War I, he had gone over the hill, and this

---

* PAL – prisoner at large, an offender restricted in movements but not confined.
† The minesweeper *Starling* (AM-64), built by the General Engineering and Dry Dock Company, Alameda, California, was launched 11 April 1942 and commissioned 21 December 1942.
‡ OD – officer of the day.

was the thing to do, so he wanted to know where do you turn yourself in. I had no idea. Even the OD didn't know.

Paul Stillwell: I wonder why he had the pang of conscience after all this time?

John Vaessen: Coming to the naval base and seeing all these guys.

Paul Stillwell: What sort of accommodations did they have at Goat Island when you reported in?

John Vaessen: Lousy.

Paul Stillwell: Were they actual barracks?

John Vaessen: They had a barracks. They put bunks in later. I went home every night because I had no uniform.

Paul Stillwell: What did you do during the daytime? Was it a training period?

John Vaessen: We kind of stood around there. No, no training.

Paul Stillwell: What was the purpose of your being there?

John Vaessen: We were in the Navy! Who knows? The Navy does a lot of crazy things. This is not unusual. [Laughter]

Paul Stillwell: How long were you there before you got your uniforms?

John Vaessen: I didn't get that until we went to L.A. We were on the train. They put us aboard the train.

John B. Vaessen Interview (6/11/87) – Page 23

Paul Stillwell: This is in the spring of 1941?

John Vaessen: Yes. I was there about five or six days at Goat Island, and then they put a whole bunch of us on the train and we went down. There was a baseball team on the same car with us.

Paul Stillwell: Whose baseball team?

John Vaessen: The San Francisco Seals. That was kind of interesting with all those types, of course.

Paul Stillwell: Pacific Coast League.

John Vaessen: Yes, one of the better teams. They really played ball.

Paul Stillwell: Joe DiMaggio had come out of that team a few years earlier.

John Vaessen: No, I don't think he was in that bunch.

Paul Stillwell: He had been there earlier.

John Vaessen: Yes, he probably was. There was a movie star on the train too. Lupe Velez, I think it was. Anyway, all the guys were ga-ga over her.

Paul Stillwell: Where did you report in at Los Angeles?

John Vaessen: We got to the train station, and they didn't have any transportation, so I guess whoever was in charge of it found out how were we going to get out to this Chavez Ravine. Lilac Terrace is the address. So they battered around what to do. The Navy couldn't supply transportation, so somebody suggested we all chip in a dime and we get a cab. There were two or three cabs, and they drove us out. That's how we got there. We paid our own way.

Paul Stillwell: What sort of facility did you report to?

John Vaessen: It was pretty nice.

Paul Stillwell: Was this the big reserve center?

John Vaessen: Yes.

Paul Stillwell: I think that had been built by the WPA.*

John Vaessen: It was formerly a brickyard. They used that for the incinerator.

Paul Stillwell: What happened when you got there?

John Vaessen: That's where we were issued a uniform.

Paul Stillwell: Did they have a barracks for you to stay there?

John Vaessen: Yes, they had a place. We went through the training, like at midnight guarding the clothesline and all that kind of crap.

Paul Stillwell: Was this considered boot camp?†

---

* WPA – Works Progress Administration, a Depression-relief agency that sometimes created make-work projects in order to stimulate employment.
† "Boot" is a slang term for a newly enlisted sailor or Marine. Recruit training is known as boot camp.

John Vaessen: Kind of like. Then they thought they were going to make a signalman out of me, and, geez, I was going batty looking at that stuff. That wasn't my line at all.

Paul Stillwell: Did they have any sort of tests or interviews to determine your civilian specialties?

John Vaessen: No, not that I know of. A lot of these guys, they had a radio thing there, and they were all hams. They were pretty good at it. This fit right in with them, but I guess they needed signalmen too. The rest of us didn't have any radio training. They were going to do that with them.

Paul Stillwell: How demanding was the military discipline in that environment?

John Vaessen: I guess the most demanding that I had encountered. Like they got us up at midnight once because somebody had swabbed the floor, and a piece of swab come loose and stuck around the bed. Everybody got up, and one guy, they asked him if he washed his white clothes, and he said he did, and they didn't think so, so everybody marched across, and then he got to wash it. You know, that kind of stuff.

Paul Stillwell: Sort of Mickey Mouse type treatment.

John Vaessen: Yes, all that kind of—

Paul Stillwell: Were there classroom training sessions to give you some orientation about the Navy?

John Vaessen: Not about the Navy. They wanted all this signal stuff, and I just was a failure at that. So they decided after so many weeks that I would be shipped to San Diego for assignment.

Paul Stillwell: How long would you say that period lasted in Los Angeles?

John Vaessen: That was about a month, but we had all this on the grinder, you know, with the rifle and you do this, the salute, and all that kind of stuff.*

Paul Stillwell: It sounds very similar to boot camp.

John Vaessen: Yes, it's like boot camp. Put it on your right shoulder, present arms, about face, and all that kind of stuff.

Paul Stillwell: Did you feel a sense of frustration that you weren't catching on with the signaling?

John Vaessen: I knew I wasn't going to be. I had made up my mind. I'm not a stubborn Dutchman for nothing. [Laughter] That wasn't for me. They ain't going to railroad me into that.

Paul Stillwell: This wasn't a deliberate thing on your part, was it?

John Vaessen: Well, you can look at it that way. [Laughter]

Paul Stillwell: Oh, you can? Did you have a chance to express a preference, though?

John Vaessen: No, absolutely not.

Paul Stillwell: So what happened once you got to San Diego?

---

* The term grinder refers to a large paved area at a shore facility, used for parades, drills, and inspections.

John Vaessen: We were put in the receiving station.

I must tell you one funny thing before we get to San Diego. At this reserve center, they brought a bunch of old-timers that had come back into the Navy, had retired or whatever, and they came back. They were kind of running the show. So they had everything on a record, the wake-up call and chow, that kind of thing. So one Sunday morning, it was before reveille, the guy played liberty. He played that record. He said, "All my life I wanted to do that." [Laughter] He said, "Before anything else." So he did it. It wasn't that funny to us, but the old-timers, boy, they thought that was the last word!

Paul Stillwell: That was in Los Angeles?

John Vaessen: That was in Los Angeles, yes.

Paul Stillwell: When you got down to San Diego, did they make you pay your own transportation again?

John Vaessen: No, no, they took us down on a train again, and they met us. We were met at the gate, and this fellow that I later got to serve aboard ship with, Ed Maurenden, he was at the gate. He was a radioman, a ham. He was good at it. He had graduated from this school a month or two before. So there was quite a bunch of us, we all looked like a bunch of boots, and he says, "Okay, all line up. What do you do now? Oh, yeah, at ease. Just follow me." [Laughter] So we went over and reported to the barracks, where we were going to stay.

Paul Stillwell: This was at the receiving station.

John Vaessen: Receiving station.

Paul Stillwell: It was actually barracks; not a ship?

]John Vaessen: Barracks.

Paul Stillwell: Did they have bunks or hammocks?

John Vaessen: Bunks. There was a lot of construction going on, lots of things going on there.

Paul Stillwell: Was this at 32nd Street, where the fleet was?

John Vaessen: Near National City. While we were there, this Captain McCandless—Captain Mac, as they called him—he was one of a kind.* You never knew what he was going to do. He called us the bluejackets. That's not sailors to him; bluejackets. So the only thing he required, that you line up and you'd march to [unclear], and everybody works. Everybody. East Side Brewery was right alongside of it, and they were bringing in dirt. They were fixing a parking lot. They had to haul it out of the bay, I guess, and there were all these seashells. So he had all of us working there to pick the shells out, put them in a bag, and carry them away. So he'd come out and he says, "Everybody working, follow me." So we'd go trotting down to the canteen, and we all had Cokes or Pepsis or whatever they had—on him. That's the way he was.

Paul Stillwell: He was in charge, I think, of the mothballed destroyers there at San Diego.

John Vaessen: They were taking yachts and turning them over to naval use at that time.

---

* The commanding officer of the destroyer base was Captain Byron McCandless, USN (Ret.). He had taken command in 1937, transitioned to the retired list in 1940, but remained in command until 8 September 1945, shortly after the end of World War II. He was promoted to the rank of commodore on the retired list. The frigate USS *McCandless* (FF-1084) was named in honor of the commodore and his son, Rear Admiral Bruce McCandless, USN (Ret.).

Paul Stillwell: I think it was known as Red Lead Row, because they had that preservative.*

John Vaessen: Yes, probably. I don't know. Anyway, he was all over the place. Like one night he went out to the sentry on duty, and he says, "Let me see your rifle." So the guy handed it to him. Then he chews his ass off. He says, "You never give your rifle." And he took it and fired a shot. He said, "What are you going to do now?" [Laughter] That's the kind of things he did.

Paul Stillwell: That makes a much more vivid impression on a guy than just telling him.

John Vaessen: Yes. He says, "What are you going to say when people call up?"

Paul Stillwell: What work did you do during the daytime? Was it mostly make-work?

John Vaessen: Yes, but he wanted everybody to be doing something, so you did all kinds. It wasn't sweeping and washing. But the WPA was still in existence then, and they were putting up a lot of these buildings.

Paul Stillwell: Were you involved in construction at that point?

John Vaessen: No, we weren't involved in that. Like I said, they were spreading this dirt out. Anyway, we found out we could sneak over by the brewery, the East Side Brewery, and the guy in the brewery would give us a little beer here and there. So we didn't mind working on that side of the base. [Laughter]

Paul Stillwell: How much liberty did you have as unrated men?

---

* Red lead is the nickname for an orange-colored anti-corrosive primer paint applied to bare metal before the regular paint is put on.

John Vaessen: Not bad.

Paul Stillwell: Had you had it all along at Goat Island and at Los Angeles, as well?

John Vaessen: At Goat Island, because I can't ever remember sleeping there, because they didn't have bunks then, I know that. Later on they did, and they were made of wood, because there was a metal shortage. When I came back to put the *Starling* in commission, I was there.

Paul Stillwell: What sorts of things did you do on liberty in San Diego?

John Vaessen: We'd go downtown. Like most sailors, you'd get a couple of drinks. One time we left the base. Who was I with? I think it was with Wallis or Hinkle, one of them, that went aboard the *Utah* with me later, and we walked through the Navy housing project. We'd see a couple of little kids come running out, "Daddy! Daddy! Daddy!"

I said, "Gee, I haven't been here before." But the uniform is what they saw, you know. [Laughter] And any sailor looked like daddy to them.

Paul Stillwell: At what point had you gotten on the payroll? Was that in Los Angeles?

John Vaessen: Los Angeles. We got paid there.

Paul Stillwell: Was this the standard $21.00 a month?

John Vaessen: Yes.

Paul Stillwell: How far could you stretch that on liberty in those days?

John Vaessen: A weekend would do it.

Paul Stillwell: How did you spend the rest of the month?

John Vaessen: You didn't go anywhere. I think they only let us out on weekends. I'm not familiar with that. We'd hitch a ride into town. This is in L.A. People were very patriotic then, and this woman picked up—I've forgotten where it was—well, another guy and I, and took us right downtown. She was glad to give us a ride and all that kind of stuff. We got out and looked, and she had dogs in the back; we were covered with dog hair. We spent an hour brushing that stuff off.

Paul Stillwell: So that's how you paid for your ride.

John Vaessen: Yes. [Laughter]

Paul Stillwell: What sorts of things did you do during your off-duty hours in the barracks when you couldn't afford to go on liberty?

John Vaessen: We had rope yarn Sunday. I don't know if they still have that or not. That's when you're supposed to wash your hammock.

Paul Stillwell: Wednesday afternoon.

John Vaessen: Yes. You are familiar with it. Just checking.

Paul Stillwell: I think they compensated for that by the fact that you were on duty on Saturday morning and probably had inspection at that time.

John Vaessen: Oh, yes, that's always a drag.

Paul Stillwell: Did you play cards and so forth in the barracks?

John Vaessen: Some did. I didn't, but some did. Usually it would be a bull session. Everybody tells you about their home towns. That always was fun.

Paul Stillwell: How much did you keep in contact with your mother during this period?

John Vaessen: I used to write her fairly often.

Paul Stillwell: Was she supportive of your going into the Navy?

John Vaessen: Well, as supportive as she could be. I mean, no mother really likes that. Of course, there was no war going on then, but there were threats.

Paul Stillwell: Was there any specific training connected with the time in San Diego?

John Vaessen: No training. I mean, I don't even remember if we had inspection. I can't remember. It just fades away.

Paul Stillwell: What recollections do you have of the Navy chow there?

John Vaessen: Good. Very good. Fact is, Captain Mac, as they called him, he had to make a phone call to Washington every couple of days before he was going over his budget. He had a standard rule, and he would get up and make announcements at noontime, you know, and he'd say, "Today is payday, so tomorrow there will be tomato juice." And there was. For hangovers. That kind of stuff. Then he read off an announcement they were opening a USO, so he read all this announcement, the street and the people in charge, and all that kind of stuff.* But he said, "What

---

* USO – United Services Organization is a group of U.S. civilians who put on entertainment programs for service personnel and provide hospitality for them in many parts of the world.

they really need is more pool rooms." [Laughter] That's the way he was, you know.

Paul Stillwell: Any other memories you have specifically of him?

John Vaessen: Yes. Everybody, when you go onto a base, is supposed to know who the commanding officer is. That is a requirement. So there's a couple of guys. He gets behind where they're serving chow, I think it was soup or potatoes or something, and he's serving it. So he's dishing it out to a couple of guys, and they're not acknowledging him. So he has the Marines take them away because they didn't know who he was.

Paul Stillwell: He was not dressed in his captain's uniform?

John Vaessen: No. He had his coat off and his hat, and that's all you could see behind the service line.

Paul Stillwell: So he just had on his white shirt?

John Vaessen: They asked for some more food or something to cause a controversy. So, anyhow, he had the Marines take this guy away.

Paul Stillwell: Was there any gambling in the barracks?

John Vaessen: Oh, yes, the galloping dominoes.

Paul Stillwell: Any loan sharking?

John Vaessen: Yes, there was seven for five or six for five; I've forgotten how it was.*

Paul Stillwell: What was your mood at that point? Were you eager to get on with it and get away from this marking time?

John Vaessen: Not particularly, because the food was good and the conditions were good. It was a nice, sunny, warm place.

Paul Stillwell: It sounds as if it wasn't very demanding either.

John Vaessen: Well, no, people coming and going all the time. So eventually I was given a job as mess cook, but I was in the chiefs' quarters at the scullery. That's where I met this fellow Scarborough. I've never heard or seen of him since, but anyway, he says, "Oh, I'm trying my damnedest to get on the *Utah*."

Paul Stillwell: Was he a chief petty officer?

John Vaessen: No, he was in the scullery.

Paul Stillwell: He was a mess cook also.

John Vaessen: Yes. He says, "I want to get on the *Utah*." He had a relative or somebody on there he knew.
    So I said, "What is the *Utah*?"
    Well, he says, "They just swing around in the harbor. They don't go anywhere."

---

* For example, if a sailor borrowed $5.00, he would have to pay back $7.00 the next payday.

So, of course, a couple of days go by, and my name comes up assigned to the USS *Utah*. I didn't know whether he was going or not, because I didn't see him, because it changes pretty rapidly.

Paul Stillwell: Had you had anything to do with bringing that assignment about?

John Vaessen: No. One day they called us over, and you go to a yeoman and you tell a ship's preference, which never works. So I had a friend who lived across the street in Sonoma that was on a tanker, and he was on the *Cimarron*, I think it was, so I thought, you've got to get around there, that would be a pretty good deal. But you never get what you asked for, so I was assigned to the *Utah*. I had to inquire what it was. But this fellow Scarborough, he knew what it was, and he said, "They swing around the hook in San Pedro," I guess it was.

Paul Stillwell: By that point, the fleet had already gone out to Pearl, hadn't it?

John Vaessen: No. Some of the ships had, I guess.[*]

Paul Stillwell: What was your rate in the summer of 1941?

John Vaessen: I was seaman first at that time, because you can't be converted until you're assigned to something. No, wait a minute. Where did I get it changed? I don't know if it was aboard the *Utah* or not. I can't remember.

Anyway, I get assigned to the *Utah*.[†] There was Charlie Hinkle, Gerald

---

[*] In October 1939 the Navy Department directed the establishment of a Hawaiian Detachment of the U.S. Fleet, which was then based in California. In the spring of 1940 the bulk of the fleet remained in Hawaii after going there for Fleet Problem XXI. Thus the major ships of the U.S. Pacific Fleet were operating out of Pearl Harbor at the time the Japanese struck in December 1941.

[†] USS *Utah* (BB-31) was commissioned as a *Florida*-class battleship in August 1911. She had a standard displacement of 21,825 tons, was 522 feet long, and 88 feet in the beam. Her top speed was 21 knots. Her main battery comprised ten 12-inch guns. In 1931-32 she was converted to a mobile target ship. On 1 July 1931 her hull number changed to AG-16. She also served as a training ship for gunnery. She was eventually sunk at Pearl Harbor during the Japanese attack in December 1941.

Strints, John Wallis, and I, and there was other people. There were some rated people, and there was a guy named Rocholdt from Porterville, and he had a little friend with him, too, and they both had musical instruments. They said, "Oh, boy, we're getting on a ship with a band!" Wanted to play in the band in the worst way. But there were other people besides me, and there was, I think, a chief boatswain's mate in charge, because he was at the receiving station where they gathered us all. He was a pretty rough-looking guy, but he was as good as they come. So he was in charge.

Paul Stillwell: You were gathered together into a draft?

John Vaessen: Yes, a draft.* So they put us on a truck and drove to San Pedro, and took most of the day to get there. It was in the late evening.

Paul Stillwell: What month would that have been? Was that September?

John Vaessen: That was in September, yes. It was pretty late in the evening. San Pedro, I think it was. There was a little YMCA there, so we went in there and somebody made arrangements. After a while, a launch came along to take us aboard the *Utah*, and it was anchored way out. So we all get on there, and gee, the mist is blowing and it's cold, the sea air is making this damp and everything. By the time we get to the ship, it's dark and the movies are going on. They've got this little, narrow gangway to walk up, and you've got this big seabag on your shoulder. So we struggled up there, finally get to the top. So at last we can walk on the deck. Oh, no, you've got to climb up all this timber. It was stacked on the deck, but they had stacked it wherever a hatch was, so you had to crawl over that and around—slivers. I don't know. Rough timber. So we had to be careful there.

---

* "Draft" is a term used to describe a group of service personnel traveling together to the same destination.

Paul Stillwell: How big were these pieces? Two-by-fours, maybe?

John Vaessen: Oh, no, they were 8-by-12, 20, 22 foot long, whatever they come. Very thick timbers.

Paul Stillwell: So those are pretty heavy pieces of wood.

John Vaessen: Yes, they were. So then they said, "Oh, the movie's going on. You'll have to go behind the movie screen." So that meant another detour.

Paul Stillwell: Was the movie out on the fantail?

John Vaessen: It was on topside. I don't know whether it was the fantail or the bow. Damned if I know. All these guys are watching the movie. We had to go behind the screen.

Paul Stillwell: It was up on the weather deck, in any case.

John Vaessen: Yes, it was out in the weather. Everybody's bundled up, but they're watching the flick. So finally, we get to the hatch to go down where it was light and you could see, by the time we got there, that seabag was heavy and digging into your shoulder. Oh, wow! So we were escorted to where our division was to be. Somehow or other, they were going to make the electrician strikers, but I don't know where that came up.*

Paul Stillwell: Had you mentioned to anybody your experience?

John Vaessen: I must have. I don't know. I can't recall. Anyway, there was the

---

* A striker is a non-rated enlisted man or woman officially designated as being in training for a specific petty officer rating.

four of us were brought down to the compartment and showed where we were going to sleep and where to put our hammocks and sea bags and all that stuff. There was no bunks on that ship. So they said, "Take your sea bag down below and put it in the hammock netting." So this one guy, he says, "This is where Dillinger, when he was on the *Utah*, this is where he put his. He won't mind at all if you use his space."*

Paul Stillwell: You mean John Dillinger, the criminal?

John Vaessen: Yes. He was on the *Utah*.

Paul Stillwell: He'd been in the Navy?

John Vaessen: Yes, and he went over the hill. [Laughter] So we were in good company.

Paul Stillwell: Had you ever slept in a hammock before?

John Vaessen: That was the first and last time.

Paul Stillwell: I hear it takes some practice to get used to that.

John Vaessen: John Wallis and I—and I don't know where Strints and Hinkle went, I think they slept on the deck. There were some lockers around on the other side. Anyway, in the morning, at 5:30 here comes the master-at-arms with a club, and I can still feel where he hit me. Boy, we come flying out of those hammocks, and we said, "What in the hell are we getting up so early for?"

He said, "To get your coffee." So anyhow, we got up.

---

* John Dillinger, a notorious bank robber and killer in the 1930s, had joined the Navy in 1923 and was assigned to the *Utah* as a fireman third class. He had disciplinary problems as a sailor and eventually deserted.

The next night we slept on the deck. No rapping in the ass for us.

Paul Stillwell: Was that accompanied by reveille on the bugle?

John Vaessen: I don't remember. Anyway, he came through to make sure we got up. We had family-style food there.

Paul Stillwell: I'd be interested in hearing about that arrangement. Did you have an individual mess in your compartment?

John Vaessen: Yes. They called it family style, and you had a mess captain, usually the senior ranking guy would sit up, and they would come down from the galley with all the food in tureens. Do they use that anymore or not?

Paul Stillwell: No, they've got general messes now, cafeteria style.

John Vaessen: Anyway, it comes in a tureen, pots, three or four, and they've got a little clamp that holds, so they can bring down the potatoes and vegetables and that kind of stuff. Then he would bring down a plate of meat or whatever it was to be. Then the mess captain would take it and pass it down the table. Being the junior members, we got to sit at the end.

Paul Stillwell: Was the seating strictly in order of seniority?

John Vaessen: Yes. So we got all the Cadota figs we wanted, but nothing else. [Laughter]

Paul Stillwell: I find that hard to believe.

John Vaessen: Well, because these guys helped themselves before we ever got to it. Who are you going to complain to?

Paul Stillwell: How senior was the head of the mess there? Was he a first class?

John Vaessen: He was a first class, yes.

Paul Stillwell: Was he an electrician's mate?

John Vaessen: Yes. I know him. I've met him since.

Paul Stillwell: What's his name? Do you recall?

John Vaessen: Perkins is his last name. There was a radio show. His name is Marion, and I don't think he likes that. What the heck did they call him? Anyway, Perkins is his last name. He was first class, I know that. He lives down near Palm Springs.

Paul Stillwell: Did the food situation improve after a bit?

John Vaessen: No, because we would go up to the canteen and buy a sandwich or something that way. At our age at that time, we could devour a lot of food.

Paul Stillwell: So you had really been better off in San Diego.

John Vaessen: Yes, I liked that better. [Laughter]

Paul Stillwell: Was there any hazing and razzing of people?

John Vaessen: We were Naval Reserve, and when I reported for duty, this Peters, I was told to report to him.[*] Being I was seaman first and the other guys were second, the three others, they told me he was rooming down below someplace, so we went up and they had a curtain with a door.

Paul Stillwell: You should explain who Peters was.

John Vaessen: He was our division officer. He was chief warrant officer, electrician. So I knocked on the door. "Who is it?"

I told him, "Reporting for duty."

"Don't need any help." We were Naval Reserve, and the Naval Reserve was not well liked.

Paul Stillwell: There were not very many reservists on active duty yet, probably.

John Vaessen: Oh, there were quite a few. There were more later, of course, but there was enough. Anyhow, these people thought that we were taking their job away, I suppose. So he didn't need any help. I said, "Well, I've got these orders to report to you."

"Well," he says, "let's see 'em." So he took a look at them, and he told us to report to Chief Cunningham or Chief Barngrover.[†] So we went there. We were assigned two divisions, to split it up and make it even, you know. Wallis and I were in one, and Hinkle and Strints in the other.

Paul Stillwell: Was this the E Division?

John Vaessen: The E Division, yes.

---

[*] Chief Electrician John L. Peters, USN.
[†] Chief Electrician's Mate John W. Barngrover, USN.

Paul Stillwell: How large a division was it?

John Vaessen: They had about 12 rated men, about six strikers, I think, something like that. I'm not sure. I saw this Chief Barngrover the last day I was in the Navy, right here on Treasure Island, even though I was first class by then, and I was a messenger again. He was a warrant officer. I don't know if he was chief or just warrant.* But anyway, he reported in, and I had to escort him. He looked at me and thought he knew me, and as soon as I saw his name, I knew him. He says, "I know. I'm going to have the mid duty." [Laughter] So, anyhow, I have never seen or heard or him since. I escorted him to where he was supposed to report him.

Paul Stillwell: Did the enlisted men in the division give you the same sort of attitude that Peters had, that you weren't really welcome?

John Vaessen: Yes, kind of. Not all of them. You always find good and bad.

Paul Stillwell: Did you develop some friendships?

John Vaessen: Oh, yes, very strong, even today.

Paul Stillwell: Did they help you break into the shipboard routine?

John Vaessen: Each striker was assigned to a rated man. I was assigned to a fellow named Ed Gurtz, and he was from Tennessee. He was supposed to show me how to stand a watch on the switchboard and other details. So this Peters, he says, "You know, we've got lots of help now." One of the jobs of the E Division were these portable lights that they plug in for the guys working in the bilges and so forth. They used to coil them up and hand them out, and they put their name down, where they're going to be. Then they'd bring them back, and if there was

---
* Barngrover eventually retired from the Navy in 1947 as a chief warrant officer-2.

damage, it was supposed to be repaired and so forth. He says, "You know, we've got these new people on there. Instead of just handing them out, they can go with them, plug them in, string them out and tie 'em up. Then we won't have so many damaged."

At this time, there was some kind of an inspection. Seems like there's always an inspection of some kind. I was down in the bilges stringing out these lights, tying them up. I don't know whether they were seamen or firemen or whatever it was, scraping and painting, that kind of work. We had blisters on the side, and they were also working on them.[*] Getting these long cords and stringing them out, you know, he didn't know that later on it was going to help me, but I didn't either.

Anyhow, I strung all these lights out, and the other fellows did the same thing. Besides we had to stand watches on the board. This Peters would come down. Occasionally he'd come down the ladder, he'd come down past the radio room, and we were down below the radio room. He would walk by, and we had one of these open switchboards. I don't know if you have seen these kind with the knife-blade switches.

Paul Stillwell: No.

John Vaessen: They had a wooden rail so you wouldn't bump into it, and you just bring it up. There would be copper like this, then the blade would fit in and close the circuit.

Paul Stillwell: It presumably had an insulated handle on the end.

John Vaessen: Yes, an insulated handle, usually wood painted black or something. But they were different sizes for the different amperage and so forth. So he would

---

[*] When the old battleships were modernized, external compartments were welded onto the ship to provide increased protection against torpedo damage. The compartments were nicknamed "blisters."

come by and he would pull one, you know. Then you'd get a call on the phone, "This is the junior officers' wardroom. We don't have any lights. What happened?" Gee, I'd look, and the switch was out. How do you explain all this? They would push a bell, and it would ring a buzzer, and you'd talk on the voice tube, go like this and this. You'd try to hear what's going on.

Paul Stillwell: Was he doing this to play a trick or to train you?

John Vaessen: I don't know. To see if we were alert, I guess. I would assume so. I don't know. Then we got to water the batteries.

Paul Stillwell: Did they have the battery-powered battle lanterns that were supposed to go on in emergencies?

John Vaessen: Didn't have that. We had a bank of batteries. There was a little room behind the ladder, coming down, around the corner from where I was. That was the little battery compartment. There were like in your car, real big. They were all put together, and that was emergency lights.

Paul Stillwell: She was an old ship, close to 30 years old at that point. Was she showing her age?

John Vaessen: The stories used to go that way. Of course, I never got around too much on it because we were always with bombing practice, and I was down below decks, so that's all I got to see. It was old-fashioned equipment, I realize that. Then we had the very latest amplidynes and guns on the ship, which I never got to see. They were covered over. If you've read any stories about it, they called them doghouses, covered them up.

Paul Stillwell: This was to protect them from the bombing?

John Vaessen: Yes.

Paul Stillwell: What do you remember about those bombing practices? Did the ship go to general quarters?

John Vaessen: No. We were mostly out on Lahaina Roads or something.* We'd go back and forth.

Paul Stillwell: Presumably the ship left San Pedro pretty soon.

John Vaessen: Yes, the next day after I got aboard. It never swung around on a hook there. [Laughter] On the way over, we hit one hell of a storm.

Paul Stillwell: How did she ride in a storm?

John Vaessen: Well, not too bad. They decided on the trip over, to try out the radio control. I guess there must have been another ship alongside that could control this. They never had taken the crew off, but it could be operated without anybody aboard, theoretically. So they tried it out, and the ship just turned around and headed back to San Pedro, so the ship was smarter than anybody aboard. [Laughter] Anyway, they tried that out.

Paul Stillwell: What could you see or hear during the bombing practice? Did you get reports over the phones of what was happening?

John Vaessen: We didn't. We were either on the switchboard. There was a long passageway with old cabling that the yard had cut off. It was fired in the coal

---

* Lahaina Roads is an area off the Hawaiian island of Maui. The U.S. Fleet often used it as an exercise area and anchorage in the years prior to World War II.

bunkers or whatnot. We would spend our time pulling that stuff out.

Paul Stillwell: So for you, a bombing practice was probably not much different from a normal underway watch.

John Vaessen: No, not too much different. But the bombing practice, we would have people from other ships or Marine or Army, and they would get in the old gun turrets. The guns were removed, and they would get in the turrets and look out whatever they look out, and when their group was dropping these little practice bombs, they had a little shell and it gave off a little puff of smoke, sometimes it would land near the vent and we'd be down there choking and coughing for five or ten minutes. But then the people in the old gun turrets would run out between. If it was today, they'd use an aerosol can, but they would paint around and put it on a chart or whatever, to give the guys a record of some kind of how good they were doing.

Paul Stillwell: This was for both Navy and Army planes?

John Vaessen: Anything. I mean, different weeks with different groups. We had the Marines one time, we had the Army, we had different carriers. This was all practice for them.

Paul Stillwell: You talk about these doghouses. These were built out of the timbers you described?

John Vaessen: No, they were metal. They covered the 1.1 guns.[*] Down in the amplidyne room, the next room next to me, was always amplidyne motors which

---

[*] Early in World War II, a number of U.S. Navy ships were outfitted with 1.1-inch antiaircraft guns. But they were unreliable, prone to jamming, so they were soon replaced by better guns.

controlled all the swinging of the guns, to keep them coordinated.

Paul Stillwell: What was the purpose of the timbers?

John Vaessen: These little bombs would come through the deck. Sometimes they did. One time the mess tables we had would be hung up on the ceiling in kind of racks. I don't know if you've seen these folding tables we used.

Paul Stillwell: Right. Triced up to the overhead.

John Vaessen: Yes. They were stuck on the overhead. Mess cooks would leave the ketchup and the mustard and that kind of stuff on the tables. One time one came through, and it just splattered all over the place. So it would come between the timbers, because they didn't cross them; they just laid it out. Sea action or something would move it, and it would be a little gap. A guy would hit a critical spot.

Paul Stillwell: Presumably they provided protection most of the time.

John Vaessen: Yes, most of the time they did.

Paul Stillwell: How did you spend your time when you weren't on watch, when one of these practices wasn't taking place?

John Vaessen: Oh, they always had us doing something.

Paul Stillwell: Such as?

John Vaessen: Repairing these portable lights, sound-powered phones. No, wait a minute. I don't think we had sound-powered phones. I don't remember. Then we would go in hauling all this old stuff out, the old barbettes and stuff, because there was nothing down in there.

Paul Stillwell: Were you involved in chipping and painting and cleaning?

John Vaessen: No, I never got in on that.

Paul Stillwell: Did you get involved in any mess cooking on board the ship?

John Vaessen: No, because they went alphabetical. I'm down in the V's. [Laughter]

Paul Stillwell: How did you spend your off-duty time? Did you gradually get accepted into this group of electricians?

John Vaessen: Some of them. Some were very, very nice, to this day.

Paul Stillwell: Was it again the bull sessions that you remembered from San Diego and that sort of thing?

John Vaessen: Yes, a lot of that. Of course, everybody was looking for their mail.

Paul Stillwell: Were you in and out of Pearl Harbor during this time?

John Vaessen: We'd go in practically every weekend, and we always tied up at a different place. We had no assigned place. Just the day it got hit happened to be in a carrier's berth. I guess the timbers looked like a carrier at a quick glance, so they wasted the torpedoes on that.

Paul Stillwell: Were you usually moored at Ford Island, or more often anchored out?

John Vaessen: One time we were at Ten-Ten Dock.* We were at all the different berths. Every week it would be a different place. Whatever ship wasn't coming in, we would take their berth, and they were sure they weren't coming.

Paul Stillwell: Were you gradually learning more and more about being an electrician as the time passed?

John Vaessen: Yes, as much as you could use on there. We would service the vents, and it was all DC, you know.† You don't hardly find DC these days. That's a rare thing.

Paul Stillwell: How much formality was there, say, between you as a junior enlisted man and a senior petty officer and commissioned officers?

John Vaessen: Well, I never got to really meet any of them, except in your own division. I mean, it's like a little colony here and another little colony there.

Paul Stillwell: Did Peters gradually warm up?

John Vaessen: No. But I'll tell you what he did do. The World Series was on, and he stationed one guy to listen to the radio. He was a sports nut from way back. He had this one guy, this was his duty, to listen to the radio, and every move that happened, if a man got on base or if a guy got a hit, who was up and what was the score, to report to him.

---

* Ten-Ten Dock, which was part of the Pearl Harbor Navy Yard, was so named because it was 1,010 feet long.
† DC – direct current.

Paul Stillwell: It was the Yankees and Dodgers that year.

John Vaessen: I have no idea who it was. I didn't get suckered in on that.

Paul Stillwell: Peters wasn't privileged to listen himself, was that it?

John Vaessen: I guess he had to be up on top or something, I don't know.

Paul Stillwell: What do you remember about your liberty there in Pearl Harbor?

John Vaessen: I used to go over and see my friend Sam Budnau. He was at the receiving station, and he was supposed to go to Johnston Island when they got a big enough group together, to go to radar. He says, "Vass, what the hell is that?"

I says, "I have no idea."

Paul Stillwell: It was a very closely held secret at that point.

John Vaessen: Yes. He would ask around. People would say, "You'll find out." But he never made it, I mean, didn't get to go there.

Paul Stillwell: How stringent were the officers of the deck in inspecting the uniforms of liberty personnel?

John Vaessen: Oh! Some were good, and you'd get to learn who is and isn't. Like this Lieutenant Little, he was on the ship—he was killed—and he was the toughest of all.[*]

Paul Stillwell: What sort of things would he talk about?

---

[*] Lieutenant (junior grade) John G. Little III, USN.

John Vaessen: Before you'd go over, on an old ship like that, you'd come up through the hatches and everything, and you wore whites. You'd get a little black spot. He would turn you back. So the people you'd get to know on the ships said, "Always carry your chalk with you." There's always ways of getting around it.

Paul Stillwell: Chalk over the black spot.

John Vaessen: Yes.

Paul Stillwell: And you might keep an eye out, too, so that you'd go ashore when some of the less strict guys were on.

John Vaessen: Well, you never knew who was up there until you got there.

Paul Stillwell: I would presume there were watch bills posted.

John Vaessen: We had to wear undress blues to go on top.

Paul Stillwell: Then there were liberty launches to take you ashore?

John Vaessen: Yes. We had the 50-foot motor launches. I guess all the other ships of the fleet had done away with them. We had a small crew, so we always carried people back to the other ships if we were way on the other side.

Paul Stillwell: You say a small crew. How large do you remember it being?

John Vaessen: I'd say 600 would be a round number. I don't know.

Paul Stillwell: Which is certainly fewer than a full battleship.

John Vaessen: Yes, much less. We had lots of room, plenty of room.

Paul Stillwell: After a time, did you get to sleeping in a hammock?

John Vaessen: No, no, I never slept in a hammock.

Paul Stillwell: Still on the deck?

John Vaessen: Always on the deck. We got cots later on. Somebody wised us up to go down to the carpenter shop and get some cots, but somebody found the cot sticks were broken. We went down to the carpenter shop without a chit, so we got run out of there. We finally did get some cot sticks and got to sleep there. But the thing that got me was we were issued a bucket, and the bucket, you fill it with cold water, and just off of our compartment you'd step in, and it was like a shower room, and there was a trough. This is the way you'd wash your teeth and your clothes and everything else. To get hot water, you had a brass pipe you'd drop in the bucket, and you'd open the valve, steam comes in, keep putting your hand in there until it was hot enough. Then whatever you were going to do, if you were going to wash clothes or wash yourself, you'd judge your own temperature.

Paul Stillwell: So there were no showers per se?

John Vaessen: There were showers, yes. But if you went at the right time of the day, you might get a steam shower. I don't know, they turned the water off or something. You had to be very careful when you went to the shower. I went during the movies.

Paul Stillwell: How often did they have movies, every night?

John Vaessen: In port they did, yes.

Paul Stillwell: So you'd get yourself all fixed up for liberty, take the launch ashore. What happened then?

John Vaessen: Usually I'd try to meet my friend over to the receiving station to see if he had liberty, and many times he did, and sometimes he didn't. I'd hang around with him for a while. I'd go downtown for a while, and then I'd come back and they always had something that they call the Nimitz Center now, but it was the bowling alley and all that kind of stuff. I still have brochures yet. They had the battle of the bands, they had boxing matches, and all those kinds of things.

Paul Stillwell: So this was a recreational center for the fleet?

John Vaessen: Yes, fleet recreation center.

Paul Stillwell: Sounds like a pretty wholesome setup, certainly much more so than Hotel Street in Honolulu. Did you get to Hotel Street?

John Vaessen: Oh, yeah, everybody got down there.

Paul Stillwell: What do you recall about that?

John Vaessen: Nothing but white hats and lousy shore patrol. They were tough there. You had to have your sleeves down and hats so, all that kind of stuff.

Paul Stillwell: Did you have liberty expiring at midnight as a non-rated man?

John Vaessen: Yes, so you'd have to come back way before midnight because the ship, many times, was way out. If it was anchored in the yard, it wouldn't be so bad. But to make up all that time.

Paul Stillwell: How long would it take you to get back, do you think?

John Vaessen: Oh, I'd say the Pearl Harbor drivers, they ran the buses, and that's all that they went. I don't know whether they had permission to go on the base or not. But it said on the side of the bus, looked like old school buses. Or you could take the city bus, but it wasn't as reliable. These guys, you knew where they were going. I've forgot what the fare was. It wouldn't break the budget, but it would take some away.

Paul Stillwell: You've probably seen that movie *From Here to Eternity*, which had the Army guys congregating in these bars downtown too.* Did you go into them?

John Vaessen: Yes. The soldiers always amazed my friend Sam and I. We'd go to town, and they would always be sitting on the gutter with their feet in the gutter. I don't know whether they were drunk or whatever. I did try to go down one time and drink two zombies, because that's all they allowed. My legs turned to rubber. [Laughter]

Paul Stillwell: What was your main preference—beer?

John Vaessen: Yes. The beer over there wasn't that good.

Paul Stillwell: But that's all there was.

John Vaessen: Yes. You didn't name a brand. You'd just say, "Beer."

Paul Stillwell: How well did the sailors and soldiers get along together on liberty?

---

* *From Here to Eternity* was a 1953 film, based on a novel by James Jones, that depicted Army garrison life on Oahu, Hawaii, in the period just before the Japanese attacked Pearl Harbor.

John Vaessen: They kind of stayed by themselves, but the sailors outnumbered the soldiers.

Paul Stillwell: Was the shore patrol likely to haul people away if they got drunk and disorderly? Were they pretty quick about that?

John Vaessen: Yes, they were pretty strict.

Paul Stillwell: Do you have any specific recollections of incidents that took place on liberty?

John Vaessen: Yes, my friend Sam and I, we went down and had always heard of the Royal Hawaiian Hotel. So we said, "The uniform is just like a tux, isn't it?" This is what we heard. So we said, "We're going to go down and get a drink at the bar there."

Paul Stillwell: This is on Waikiki Beach.

John Vaessen: Yes. The Royal Hawaiian, the famous Royal. So we go in there. Of course, everybody's all eyes. We look at the prices, and they were pretty high. But we said, "Let's get a couple of beers." They opened up the beer, and it was warm beer; it just foamed out, and we had what was left. They didn't want us there. But that didn't bother us. We wanted to see what it was like in there. [Laughter]

Paul Stillwell: What was it like?

John Vaessen: Everybody hoity-toity.

Paul Stillwell: It turned out maybe it wasn't a tuxedo, after all.

John Vaessen: They couldn't throw us out.

Paul Stillwell: But they could discourage you.

John Vaessen: Yes. They could say, "Go some other place," like the Black Cat or something downtown, where you were accepted.

Paul Stillwell: There was a steakhouse called P.Y. Chung. Did you go there?

John Vaessen: Not P.Y. Chung. We called it Lousy Chow.

Paul Stillwell: Lau Ye Chai's. That was another one.

John Vaessen: It's still there, but it's in a different building. They tore the building down. And the Wagon Wheel Restaurant was there. It's still there, but it's a different setup.

Paul Stillwell: This was a relief, also, from your not eating so well on board ship.

John Vaessen: Yes. Then we went to Kao Kao Corner. That was kind of a drive-in. Kao Kao, what does that mean? Food and where people meet. I don't know. It means something in Hawaiian. We went roller-skating once, because we used to go up on the Russian River roller-skating. Falling down in your whites and everything didn't make them look too good. [Laughter]

Paul Stillwell: Did you go to the beach for swimming?

John Vaessen: Yes, yes, we went there. We had the G.I.-issued swimsuit, and we would rent a towel, I guess it was. We'd change and go out on the beach.

John B. Vaessen Interview (6/11/87) – Page 57

Paul Stillwell: What was your reaction? Here this was the kind of place that people paid hundreds of dollars to take an ocean liner to reach, and you were there for practically no cost. Did you enjoy that kind of atmosphere?

John Vaessen: You didn't have the money to spend to enjoy yourself like those people did. People weren't looking to serve you; they were looking to turn you away.

Paul Stillwell: Did you have a sense of resentment about that?

John Vaessen: Kind of, yes.

Paul Stillwell: How much freedom of movement did you have on board ship? Were you prohibited from places that you could go?

John Vaessen: We would go, like I had to go down to the M Division and get ice, just whatever you had to do, or up to the canteen to get a sandwich or an ice cream or something to supplement the meal.

Paul Stillwell: But you couldn't go on a tour, for example?

John Vaessen: No. I probably would be allowed. I don't know. But you just don't attempt those things.

Paul Stillwell: Did you ever get to the bridge, for example?

John Vaessen: No.

Paul Stillwell: Did you have any interest in going?

John Vaessen: I would have liked to, yeah. I'm interested in everything.

Paul Stillwell: Was there a very definite sense that you had a limited opportunity, that you had to stay in one place?

John Vaessen: That's for the people you get to know, and that's the people you hang out with. If you go up some other place, somebody would say, "What are you doing here?"

Paul Stillwell: Did that happen to you on occasion?

John Vaessen: No, because I never ventured up. You'd always be with someone else, and right away they'd want to know what you were doing there. I think we went through the junior officers' quarters once. I wanted to know what it looked like, and so we walked through like we were busy with a paper in our hands. That makes you look important.

Paul Stillwell: It's just a ruse so you can answer the question, "What are you doing here?"

Hotel Street was also notorious for the houses of prostitution. What do you remember about those?

John Vaessen: We went into them one time. There were so many people in there, so we just got out. Like you read in the thing about my friend Wallis, he wanted to go in the worst way, so I said, "I'll go with you." But he said, "Oh, to hell with this. I'm going to get a tattoo." The reason he got the tattoo, he wanted to have it on a T-shirt so it would cover.

Paul Stillwell: On his left bicep.

John Vaessen: Left or right.

Paul Stillwell: His upper arm, in any event.

John Vaessen: Yes. And the reason he wanted that, his sister was very strict, and he didn't want her to see it. But he said, "I'll look salty now." So that's the night he got it. I wanted to get some Christmas cards, because I had never seen that "Merry Christmas" in Hawaiian, so I sent one to my mother.

Paul Stillwell: This was on December sixth that this happened?

John Vaessen: Yes.

Paul Stillwell: Did the division officer or senior petty officers talk about protecting against venereal disease?

John Vaessen: Not that I remember.

Paul Stillwell: How much opportunity, if any, did you have to meet girls over there?

John Vaessen: Very little. There wasn't that many, except for Hotel Street.

Paul Stillwell: That's kind of a frustrating environment to put a young sailor in.

John Vaessen: You know, I was in one place, and there was a real old woman, and she said that she wanted to get back to the States. She had a bar on Market Street in San Francisco. I had mentioned San Francisco. I knew my way around there, and she wanted to know how things were there. I was trying to figure where this place was; I didn't even know.

Paul Stillwell: You were older, I would presume, than a number of the sailors on board.

John Vaessen: Yes, I was in my 20s.

Paul Stillwell: Did you get treated with more respect, would you say, than they did, as a result?

John Vaessen: No, I wouldn't think so. I was a little higher rated, fireman second class. There was some third class, though.

Paul Stillwell: Did you at that time do any studying toward becoming a petty officer? Were there training courses?

John Vaessen: No, nothing like that.

Paul Stillwell: What did you have to look forward to in the way of advancement?

John Vaessen: After the bombing practice, we were to go to the navy yard and give all this timber to the yard, and they were to cut it up for whatever use they wanted. There were so many stories. We were to go to Guam or Midway or someplace to pick up the Marines. Of course, all these things never happened. Other people said we would pick them up and bring them back, we'd be in the States for liberty by Christmastime. Then there would be other things going on. Of course, all that never came about.

Paul Stillwell: The *Utah*, in the late '30s, had been an antiaircraft gunnery training ship. Did she have any of that role during the time you were on board?

John Vaessen: It was there, and they had put the latest on there. But these doghouses were special steel, just like a doghouse, a steel house, covering the guns to protect them from the bombing practice.

Paul Stillwell: But did they also have antiaircraft gunnery training?

John Vaessen: Yes, it was coming up. It was next.

Paul Stillwell: But was it actually done while you were on board?

John Vaessen: No, not while I was there. Of course, I got on in San Pedro and got off in Hawaii, and had been in the shipyard up in Bremerton. Then they came down and were going out. They had been doing this for a couple of years, I guess.

Paul Stillwell: I have seen a picture with an article that you showed me from the *Proceedings* when she was being repainted from the light gray prewar color into the dark gray.[*] Was she dark gray then, by December '41?

John Vaessen: I guess.

Paul Stillwell: What do you remember of the officers? You had the executive officer who was a former enlisted man. Did you have any contact with him?

John Vaessen: Not before. After, yes.

Paul Stillwell: This was Commander Warris?[†]

John Vaessen: Yes.

---

[*] Michael S. Eldredge, "The Other Side of the Island: USS *Utah* at Pearl Harbor," *U.S. Naval Institute Proceedings*, December 1976, page 52.
[†] Commander John F. Warris, USN.

Paul Stillwell: What kind of reputation did he have?

John Vaessen: Very good.

Paul Stillwell: And what about Captain Steele?*

Paul Stillwell: Not very good.

Paul Stillwell: Why not?

John Vaessen: I don't know. I never met the man.

Paul Stillwell: What had you heard about him?

John Vaessen: Oh, you'd hear little rumbles here and there.

Paul Stillwell: Such as?

John Vaessen: I don't know, but derogatory.

Paul Stillwell: Was it about his personality?

John Vaessen: Could be.

Paul Stillwell: I gather that he was a very remote figure, then, to a non-rated man.

John Vaessen: Yes. I mean, I never saw the man. I wouldn't know if I saw him today.

---

* Commander James M. Steele, USN, was the commanding officer.

Paul Stillwell: You didn't even physically see him?

John Vaessen: No, not to my knowledge. We never had inspections and those kinds of things.

Paul Stillwell: I wonder why not. That was an institution.

John Vaessen: Well, because they had all this bombing practice, and you've got to get all these people in while they're in port, and the time for ceremony is later, which is the way it should be.

Paul Stillwell: So the inspections of the personnel were really limited to these liberty ports, it sounds like.

John Vaessen: Yes, that's all.

Paul Stillwell: You and Wallis went out on the sixth of December, and he got his tattoo. Did you go along with him?

John Vaessen: Yes. We were in the same liberty section. I bought the Christmas card, like the photocopy there, and I mailed it to my mother.

Paul Stillwell: Did you have any interest in getting a tattoo yourself?

John Vaessen: No. He wanted to know if he should have a few drinks first. I said, "That's up to you." Then he finally went through with it. He didn't know that the next day he'd be swimming in oil and salt water. [Laughter] I distinctly remember the guy saying, "Don't take a shower. Don't touch it for at least two or three days."

"Okay, I won't do it. I won't do that. No, I won't." A few hours later, he dove over the side.

Paul Stillwell: How late did you stay out that night on Saturday, the sixth of December?

John Vaessen: I guess it was 9:30 or 10:00 because we had to catch the bus back.

Paul Stillwell: But you probably didn't get back then much before midnight.

John Vaessen: No, because we were way on the other side. One time we tied up at Ten-Ten Dock, which was a breeze.

Paul Stillwell: You didn't even need the liberty launch for that.

John Vaessen: No. But this time we were way out, way on the other side.

Paul Stillwell: On the opposite side of Ford Island from the battleships.*

John Vaessen: Yes.

Paul Stillwell: How long a boat ride would that have been?

John Vaessen: An hour.

Paul Stillwell: Did you stop at other ships on the way?

John Vaessen: Yes, we usually delivered some people, because we had lots of

---

* Ford Island is in the middle of Pearl Harbor, Hawaii. At the time it was the site of a naval air station.

capacity.

Paul Stillwell: So you would be the last stop then?

John Vaessen: Yes, we were there. The coxswain would holler out, you know, what ship he's going by. They were very good about picking up people from other ships, because it all took time, though.

Paul Stillwell: Sure. Did you have the opportunity to sleep late on a Sunday morning?

John Vaessen: I think instead of 5:30, it might have been 6:00. Not very much.

Paul Stillwell: What do you remember about getting up that morning, the seventh of December, 1941?

John Vaessen: I knew I had the watch at 8:00 o'clock, and naval custom says that you relieve the man 15 minutes before the hour. So about 15 minutes before, I'm at the top of the hatch, and I'm going down. My friend Roy Sunlight tells me, "You can't go that way. You'll have to go the old way."

Paul Stillwell: Was he a petty officer?

John Vaessen: He was third class or a striker; I'm not sure.

Paul Stillwell: And what was the reason that you couldn't go the usual way to your watch station?

John Vaessen: Because he had dogged 'em down, and he had a lot of it painted, and he had some more to do.*

Paul Stillwell: Was that unusual to do painting on a Sunday?

John Vaessen: He wanted to touch up some things that he couldn't get to before.

Paul Stillwell: Had you had breakfast and gone through the usual morning activities?

John Vaessen: Yes, I had that. I guess about a quarter to, I went around and down, and I relieved this Joe Barda, and he says, "Oh, today, while you're on watch, we've got these damage control bags." They were canvas bags with a flashlight in them, a voltage tester, some fuses, tape, and extra batteries, stuff in case of damage on the ship. The electrician's duty in our division is to bring that to the damage party.

Paul Stillwell: Had you been through damage control drills?

John Vaessen: No. I was just to replace the batteries in all the flashlights, and that's what I was doing. They were in a little room right by the blister open.

Paul Stillwell: How far down in the ship were you when you were at your watch station?

John Vaessen: I'd say it was below the waterline.

---

* In this context a dog is a metal fitting used to close a hatch or watertight door. Typically it takes a number of dogs per hatch to provide the necessary watertight seal.

Paul Stillwell: Was it maybe the third deck?

John Vaessen: There was the main deck, then there was the radio room, and then there was the electrician's space. The domino flaps were below, and they were smaller because it was the smaller part of the ship.

Paul Stillwell: Where the hull curves?

John Vaessen: Yes, that's right. We had the blisters, and they were half in and half out of the water, and they had been added to the ship, because they used to also fire torpedoes at it. I guess they didn't want to sink the ship that way, break open one of these blisters and close it off, then go in and repair it later. They were all along the ship.

Paul Stillwell: We should emphasize that these were torpedoes without warheads.

John Vaessen: Yes.

Paul Stillwell: So you were probably at about the third deck when you were on your watch station. Would that be accurate?

John Vaessen: I would say so. I wish I had a diagram where I could look sideways.

Paul Stillwell: So you got down at 7:45 and relieved Barda of the watch.

John Vaessen: Yes, and he says, "We're going to start stacking the lumber, because we're going to go over to the yard and give it to them." We had two immense cranes on the ship. I don't think a battleship normally had this. I'm not sure.

Paul Stillwell: These were used for lifting the boats out of the water?

John Vaessen: No, for lifting the lumber. So he says, "You might have to throw the switch on and activate it. Make sure and call somebody and let them know, because of more fuel and the boilers and all that kind of stuff, to accommodate all this stuff." So he says, "Change the batteries and take care of these damage control kits while you're on watch, in between readings and so forth." And he says, "I want to hurry up. I want to get a Sunday paper before the newsboy leaves. They usually come on the ship. At about 8:00 they leave."

So I say, "Okay, you go on up." Of course, he never made it.

Paul Stillwell: What happened? Where did he get caught in the meantime?

John Vaessen: I don't know. Must have been the other side of the battle grating, because he got up there, and then the ship rolled and he couldn't come back.[*]

Paul Stillwell: What was the battle grating?

John Vaessen: I don't know what deck it is. It's a reinforced deck all through the ship so your engineering spaces don't get damaged in case of a bombing.

Paul Stillwell: An armored deck?

John Vaessen: I guess it would be, yes. But this grating is real heavy. I think I told you earlier that we had to crank it up. That was our GQ station.[†] Wallis and I were assigned to that, a little hand winch, you wound it up. Then there was a little clip that would hold it for normal use, but for GQ station, we kind of went through

---

[*] At 0801 on Sunday morning, 7 December 1941, a Japanese torpedo hit the forward part of the ship, and she capsized to port. Timbers used to protect the ship during bombing practice began sliding and hampered crew members as they tried to abandon ship.
[†] GQ – general quarters, in which the ship's crew is at battle stations.

that a couple of times. We would let it down to see how heavy it was, and it was heavy. You couldn't lift it. One person could not do it.

Paul Stillwell: Did it have a cable attached to it?

John Vaessen: Yes, there was a little cable and pulley, and you'd crank it.

Paul Stillwell: What was your first awareness that something was wrong?

John Vaessen: The blister started leaking water. I heard a "thud," and the water started coming in.

Paul Stillwell: Was there any announcement over the loudspeaker?

John Vaessen: No, there couldn't be. We didn't have a loudspeaker.

Paul Stillwell: They weren't that new.

John Vaessen: No, far from it. We had these voice tubes. At 8:00 o'clock, a seaman was to come down, and we had a telephone switchboard. They had phones throughout the ship, but it only operated from 8:00 to 4:00 or 5:00, I don't know what. The switchboard was in the amplidyne room, and usually the guy from the deck force would come down there.

Paul Stillwell: Where was the amplidyne room in relation to your watch station?

John Vaessen: The center of the ship.

Paul Stillwell: Were you port or starboard?

John Vaessen: I don't know.

Paul Stillwell: But you were outboard of this amplidyne room?

John Vaessen: Yes. Yes, that was in the center of the ship.

Paul Stillwell: Did you hear any noise, other than just the water coming in?

John Vaessen: Yes, I felt a "thud." When I went down to relieve Joe Barda, I think it was the *Nevada* was just coming in.* I just saw it drifting by. I was sure that we were rammed, somebody had run into us, another ship following or something. I mean, you use your imagination; that's all you can do. I thought surely. Then, boy, another one came. That's when things started tipping up.

Paul Stillwell: How soon did you have an awareness of what really happened?

John Vaessen: It was a matter of minutes. I was going to start to write all this on the log sheet. Gee, things were happening too fast for that. So anyhow, the ship started tipping. I saw this water pouring in, and I made my way to the amplidyne room, because from there the hatch—the ship was listing pretty bad—went down to the dynamo flats. So, boy, just as I got to the doorway, the ship tipped and there were deck plates, fire extinguishers, everything loose come flying. Luckily, I was hit but no vital stuff, no punctures or anything.

Paul Stillwell: Did you grab hold of something?

John Vaessen: I grabbed hold of everything. [Laughter]

---

* The USS *Nevada* (BB-36) was the only battleship that got under way on the morning of 7 December 1941. Her crew beached the badly damaged ship near Hospital Point so she would not sink in the entrance channel and block future ship movements in and out of the harbor.

Paul Stillwell: Did you grab anything that could keep you upright?

John Vaessen: Just the rails. Anyway, I headed to this hatch down to the dynamo flats. Hell, the ship was damn near over by this time. There was only one way to go, which was to go down, which would bring me up. So I got down. The ship had completely flopped by this time, and by the hatch there were four big brass bolts that opened the hatch to get to the bilges. So I said, "Gee, this water is coming up. I've got to move out of here." As the ship was laying, the superstructure was holding it up, and then you could hear something snap, and it would settle down in the water. You could see it bumping. Of course, by then there was an air pocket formed, and I was under pressure.

As luck would have it, there was a wrench in the clip. Most of the time it's not there, but this time it was there, and I had this flashlight with me because I was putting the batteries in.

Paul Stillwell: Had the lights gone out throughout the ship?

John Vaessen: Yes. I stayed on the switchboard, and through Peters's training I knew that the lights would be the most important thing in a thing like this, so I pulled the ventilation. I didn't have the cranes in yet. Any auxiliary stuff, I was yanking that, just leaving the lights.

Paul Stillwell: You were pulling these big levers?

John Vaessen: Yes, these knife switches. The lights would brighten up, and then I'd pull another one, it would be dimming and dimming. I'd pull another one and they'd lighten up again, but pretty soon they were gone. Then the batteries started blowing up with the salt water and all that stuff. So all this stuff happened in a matter of minutes.

Paul Stillwell: Did you get any announcement on the voice tubes that the ship was under attack?

John Vaessen: No, you'd have to open it to listen.

Paul Stillwell: So you still didn't really know what was causing this?

John Vaessen: No, I had no idea.

Paul Stillwell: Were you frightened?

John Vaessen: I was scared! [Laughter] That's a dumb question.

So, anyway, I opened up the four bolts, they're brass, and the studs are capped, the nuts won't come off. I don't know if you have seen this on the old portholes maybe. The same kind of thing. Portholes maybe like on the *Queen Mary*.

Paul Stillwell: I know what you mean. It won't go off the end.

John Vaessen: You can't lose it. Anyway, I opened it up, and I went down there and opened up the hatch. There was so much asbestos where they kept it down there, I was choking on the stuff. Anyway, I crawled in there anyhow. I'd been there before. I crawled through there with the light, and there would be one of these lights where you hit it, and the damn switch would fail on you. So I crawled along, thought, "Jesus, what the hell am I going to do next?" I kept the wrench that I went down there with. Incidentally, I still have it and the flashlight that still works.

Paul Stillwell: That's amazing. How long was it that you stayed on the switchboard before you left?

John Vaessen: It wasn't very long. As long as the power was gone. I was going to look down in the dynamo flats to see if the guy was down there, but it was too late. I crawled down in there and I didn't see anybody, no one there. I talked to him later—this is 40 years later, the guy called me on the phone and tells me he was the guy on watch. His name was George Race. I never did know who was there. Nobody else seemed to know either.

So, anyhow, I crawl down in there. So I take the wrench and I rap on the bottom. I said, "Gee, it sounds like it's out of water. This is a pretty good sign." So I hit it some more. I didn't know we were at war. I mean, this was unbeknownst to me. So, anyway, I rapped on the bottom, rapped and rapped. You know, your hopes are always up, so I rapped and rapped. Gee, I got the damnedest blister on my hand, but I kept rapping anyway.

All of a sudden, I hear somebody coming back, rapping, and they spoke, but I couldn't understand them. I didn't know what they were saying. I guess they couldn't understand me either, because with an inch of metal between you, you can't hear anything. So the voices talked. Pretty soon they were gone again, so I started rapping again. Then pretty soon they were back, and some more stuff. They would rap and I would rap, and I think they were trying to locate me. I'm not sure on this.

So I rapped and I rapped and I rapped, and they would rap and rap, and it was getting closer. Then there was silence again, and then I heard, "rat-tat-tat-tat-tat-tat." I'd worked in the shipyard, and I says, "Oh, they're using an air chisel." I says, "Well, there must be somebody else in some other part of the ship. I'll just have to wait my turn." But every so often I'd give a rap to make sure they knew I was there. So I rapped and rapped. This "rat-tat-tat-tat" went on a couple of times. Then it was all silent, and then it come back and there was a voice.

All of a sudden, I see a little red spot, and it started to smoke. I thought, "Holy Christ! They must be burning a hole!" So they burned it. Of course, Hill could tell you better than I.

Paul Stillwell: You should explain who Hill is.

Paul Stillwell: William D. Hill was from the *Raleigh*, and he was sent over with a group, of which you have their names, from the *Raleigh*, because the *Utah* people, I think our chief engineer, Isquith, and others had told him, "There's somebody trapped in here," and could they help out.* Of course, they were in trouble themselves, but there's not too much they could do.

Paul Stillwell: But the *Raleigh* hadn't turned over.

John Vaessen: No, they hadn't turned over. They had sunk. I can tell you something on what happened to them too. So, anyway, I have to get this story from the people as they relayed it to me, but I have to tell you my part.

I was in there, I saw the little red spot, of course, when you see metal burning and the paint and so forth. Then it would quit. Then I'd see it again in another place. Then after a while, they burned the hole and sparks come flying out. This was the first time in my life they were required, starting on that Sunday, to wear white shorts, because we were in the tropics. This Ed Gurtz, who I was with, I didn't have any, and he said, "You can bring them to the tailor shop and they'll cut them off so you can wear them. I'll loan you mine." So he loaned me his, and of course, all the sparks coming down on me, the best shower I ever had. [Laughter]

Anyway, they would burn and it would go out and come on again, and then pretty soon they burned a circle so big.

Paul Stillwell: How big would you say? Two feet in diameter?

---

* Lieutenant Commander Solomon S. Isquith, USN. Hill was a chief petty officer on board the *Raleigh* (CL-7), a light cruiser. He has done an oral history on his Pearl Harbor experiences; the interviewer was Ronald E. Marcello of North Texas State University. Vaessen has also done an oral history for the North Texas collection.

John Vaessen: Oh, no, no, about 16 inches, an oval-shaped opening. But all the slag kept holding it up. Anyway, according to my friend Hill, his friend, Steve White, from the *Raleigh,* he was a big Swede from Idaho and he had worked in the sugar beet fields, and in those days they pulled the sugar beets out by hand, and he had muscles on him like you wouldn't believe. So he says he got a sledge hammer someplace. They're different for everything. And he pounded. One whack, and that plate come flying. Of course, I was way over in the corner. So they had one fellow there, a seaman, one of the guys there, with a bucket of water, and when they pounded the plate in, they told him to pour the water on the plate to cool off this metal. But I was already out and gone.

Paul Stillwell: You were the only person in that space?

John Vaessen: The only one.

Paul Stillwell: You told me before we turned on the tape a lot of false rumors grew up about that.

John Vaessen: I got this phone call, I'll tell you, a couple of weeks ago. I went to the *Raleigh*, and they made me an honorary member.

Paul Stillwell: You went to a reunion.

John Vaessen: A *Raleigh* reunion. I was made an honorary member. So, anyway, I get a call, after I get home, from a reporter from San Diego. He says, "I want to ask you about the *Utah*."

I said, "I don't like to give interviews to anybody. I want them eyeball to eyeball, because there's too many false stories coming out."

So he says, "Where did you get the ladder?"

I said, "The ladder?"

"Yeah," he says, "to get up to this hole they burned."

I said, "I don't know anything about a ladder."

Then he says he had read—and there's a story out—that there was ten other people with me. But then he heard they were all deceased, and why didn't I give a hand pulling them out. Well, I never knew this before. But what had happened, the *Raleigh* people said, "Who else is with you?"

I says, "No one that I know of." So they sent somebody down to look, and I guess that guy popped his head in and out a few times. People ashore, which was 60, 70 feet away, thought there was all kinds of people coming out. This is the way I look at it. I don't know. But a lot of people, what they don't know, they make up.

Paul Stillwell: How far were you from the hole to be able to get up and out?

John Vaessen: I had to crouch down.

Paul Stillwell: How big was the space you were in? Was it six feet high?

John Vaessen: Oh, no, no, I would say maybe three or four at the most. They always talk, "Oh, this old ship is so old, it's all rusted away and it's going to sink. It's all rusted." That was over an inch thick. I mean, you hear all these rumors. [Laughter]

Paul Stillwell: At that part maybe you were wishing it was a little bit rustier.

John Vaessen: Yes, I would have poked through myself.

Paul Stillwell: You said earlier, the time that you spent on the blister stringing the lights, helped you later. What did you mean by that?

John Vaessen: I knew my way around the bilges.

Paul Stillwell: This place they got through, was that in the blister or in the actual bottom of the ship?

John Vaessen: The actual bottom. My friend Hill told me, he says they laid the tank on the bilge keel when it was turned over, and that held the tank, because they didn't have that much hose. On a round bottom, you can't stand the thing up; it would keep falling over. There were two tanks, oxygen and acetylene. So it was a perfect place for that.

Paul Stillwell: I'm surprised that they switched from the pneumatic to the acetylene, because that might have taken some of the oxygen out.

John Vaessen: I imagined this. I thought that that was happening.

Paul Stillwell: But you heard a sound.

John Vaessen: That was the Japs strafing.

Paul Stillwell: So that wasn't it.

John Vaessen: No! And that's why I didn't hear any more voices for a while. The *Tangier* was there, and they realized this. The *Tangier* is a type of aircraft—

Paul Stillwell: Seaplane tender.

John Vaessen: Yes. They were firing their guns, keeping this new wave away from these guys burning the hole. So by them firing their gun, that kept the planes up high, but they still blasted their machine guns.

Paul Stillwell: How was the air in that space when you were still confined?

John Vaessen: Hot.

Paul Stillwell: Was it getting foul?

John Vaessen: I guess it was. Of course, I was the only one breathing it.

Paul Stillwell: That was to your advantage.

John Vaessen: But every time I'd look down, I'd see this stuff bubbling and a piece would break. Of course, Hill told me, burning this hole, that the pressure in there kept putting the torch out, and that's where they had the problem.

Paul Stillwell: Was there any water at all in the compartment you were in?

John Vaessen: Not at that time. I found out later that our people had come over and told him that to burn a hole there, you're taking a big chance. He says, "Why is that?"

They says, "Well, there's a powder magazine right on one side, and there's an oil bunker on the other side. You better make sure you're in the right place."

So he says he had to make a decision right then and there. He says, "If I was in there, I'd want somebody to try something." So he did.

Paul Stillwell: Not only that, but if you were in there, it was pretty likely you weren't in either a magazine or an oil tank.

John Vaessen: No, he knew that, but if he was in the wrong spot, they would all have been blown up.

Paul Stillwell: So a very courageous thing for him to have done.

John Vaessen: Very, very courageous.

Paul Stillwell: With the risk of asking another dumb question, what was your reaction when you finally got out?

John Vaessen: I come out, and he says I asked if the dynamo blew up. I don't think so, because I was in the dynamo room, and I knew that everything was all right in there. I thought we were rammed. So the coxswain in the boat, I says, "What happened?" I saw the *Raleigh* down in the water.

    He says, "We're at war!"

    I says, "Who with?" [Laughter]

    He said, "Japan."

    So they took me on the boat, took me over, and the WPA was digging a ditch for a sewer or water line, pretty deep ditch.

Paul Stillwell: Was this a boat from the *Raleigh*?

Paul Stillwell: I think it was one of the guys from ours. It must have been one of ours. I don't know. His name was Van Busker. He was the engineer on the boat. The others I don't know.

    But, anyway, they took me ashore and they said, "You'd better get in the ditch," because there were some planes coming over. So I jumped in the ditch, and there was our bugler. I knew him. I didn't know him very well.

Paul Stillwell: But you recognized him.

John Vaessen: Yes. He was a redhead; you couldn't miss him. And he looked at me and said, "Where did you come from?" [Laughter]

I says, "I come from the ship."

He says, "We all got off hours ago." [Laughter]

Paul Stillwell: You've shown me the log from the *Raleigh*, and it says that you came out, though it doesn't identify you by name, at about 11:00 o'clock.

John Vaessen: They didn't know. They went over at 11:00.

Paul Stillwell: So do you have any idea what time it was when you came out through the hole?

John Vaessen: The only thing I know, I was black and blue all over, and my clothes were a mess. They said, "Let's go over to the air station, down to the lucky bag, and see if we can find you some clothes." So they took me down to the air station, and they were putting away the trays from the noon meal. They had run through the scullery and everything, so it was afternoon. I don't know what time. I have no idea. But before that, I jumped in the ditch, and then I guess the all-clear sounded, and I crawled out. They said I should go over and have the doctor on the ship look at me.

So we went into this house, this officer's house. I found out later the name was Church. I laid on the floor there. There were four or five other guys there from the ship, none of them seriously hurt, but they required some attention. So the doctor came over and he says, "Where did you come from?"

I said, "I just got off the ship."

He said, "Did you see my dog?"

I said, "What?"

"Did you see my dog?" Well, he had been known to drink a lot, so he was imagining things.

So, anyhow, I was fit to get up and walk around, as far as that goes. But while I was laying there, this woman had an infant, and she comes out of the room, in the bedroom. I guess this must have been a dining room-kitchen combination. I can't remember. She goes to the refrigerator to get formula, and then she picks it all up, and then she walks back. This was in their house. They just took over this place as a kind of sick bay. I found out their name was Church, and I was just trying to wonder, that infant now must be in his 40s. I would sure like to know whatever happened to him. [Laughter] The first days of his or her life, whatever it is, I don't know.

Paul Stillwell: It sounds like you were pretty lucid at that point, not in the shock that probably some others were in.

John Vaessen: Maybe it hadn't taken hold yet.

Paul Stillwell: Do you recall a period that you did experience a sense of shock, of being dazed?

John Vaessen: I know we didn't sleep for about a week. You'd go to bed, but you didn't sleep.

Paul Stillwell: Why not?

John Vaessen: Nervous, I guess. But that night we didn't have any place to sleep, so Wallis and I, somebody brought us some mattress covers, and we slept under a house—I don't know which one it was—a couple of nights. We'd pull the mattress covers over us to keep the mosquitoes from biting us.

Paul Stillwell: When had you gotten together again with Wallis?

John Vaessen: That same day. He was looking for me. He wanted to know where I was. His name was John Delbert Wallis. We slept a couple of nights. We were looking for something to eat. We were getting kind of hungry. So we went down to the air station, where the mess hall was, and they said they needed water for the coffee, because rumors were out that the water was poisoned. You know, all these rumors fly all over the place. So we said, "We'll go down to the swimming pool," which the ship had tied up there. We could see it was the officers' swimming pool, and all these kids were in there. You know what kids do in the pool. So anyway, it didn't make any difference with the chlorine and everything. So we got a bucket of water. We brought it to the cook, and he says, "Well, you can have breakfast." There was a plate of beans and coffee, which was fine with us.

This is the next morning. We went down to the *Tangier*, and this other fellow showed up. I wish I knew his name. He had a pair of dungarees on, and he had a dollar bill in his hind pocket and it was soaking wet because he had swam over. He said, "Gee, I've got a dollar bill. There's five of us. I'll go over and get some Clipper stamps. You give me your name and address of whoever you want to notify." So he went over. I don't know whether we wrote it down or told him or what, but anyway, he wrote those cards. They weren't allowed to say anything. I wanted to get word home as quickly as it was possible.

Paul Stillwell: So the card that went to your mother was actually in his handwriting?

John Vaessen: Yes, that card right there and the thing in the back, you know, you could only check certain things. But he got that from the *Tangier*. They says, "Oh, while you're there, here is some bandoliers with ammunition."

He says, "How about a rifle?"

"I can't give you that."

So we all were loaded with bandoliers and ammunition, and we says, "If we're attacked, we can help somebody out, you know. We can bring them the ammunition or load the gun or whatever." That's all we could do.

That night, the December seventh night, there was some planes coming in from the mainland. I guess anything that was flying was in danger, so they were firing. There were puffs of smoke over by Barbers Point.*

Paul Stillwell: There were also some planes coming in from the *Enterprise*.†

John Vaessen: Whatever. Of course, everything was being fired at, and all these puffs. They fired any kind of gun. The puffs of smoke, they said, "Paratroopers are landing at Barbers Point." These rumors, they fly fast. So we figured we were going to be invaded. Then somebody called us aside and told us, if you're taken prisoner, what to do. I always thought it was good advice. They said, "If you're taken prisoner and you're someplace in a camp, and you take and stand on gravel, if you can find some, or sand, and keep twisting your foot, and cover your mouth when you talk, and give your escape plan in case anybody takes a picture, anybody's got a device." But we never had to use that.

Anyway, when they fired these guns, a yeoman off the *Utah*, named Pierce, a lot of the guys—not all of them—were brought to the *Argonne*, an old—

Paul Stillwell: It had been a passenger liner once.‡

John Vaessen: I don't know what it was. But anyway, they were all down below, no lights or anything, and they were all sitting around this mess table. All of a sudden, my friend Warren Upton, who lives in San Jose, he was sitting there, and Sunlight was sitting next to the guy, and he's sitting at the table, and this guy Pierce all of a sudden, he slumps over with his head on the thing. They said, "Come on, wake up. They're shooting out here." Then he said there was blood all

---

* Barbers Point was the site of a naval air station at the southwest "corner" of the island of Oahu.
† USS *Enterprise* (CV-6) was an aircraft carrier that was approaching Pearl Harbor.
‡ By 1941 the *Argonne* (AG-31) was a repair ship and served as flagship for Rear Admiral William L. Calhoun, USN, Commander Base Force.

over. So he got killed that night on the *Argonne* from our own, the *California*.* Just fired at the plane as they kept coming down, down, down, down, and then bang. Went right through the hull. I guess that must have been a thin one.

Paul Stillwell: Did you subsequently find out from your mother when she got this card that the fellow had sent?

John Vaessen: The postmaster brought it to her personally. Sonoma was a small town, and the postmaster, he got it. His name was Murphy. He ran the local newspaper also. So he made sure she got it. I think he called her up or something, I'm not sure.

Paul Stillwell: How soon was that, do you know?

John Vaessen: I don't know. On a Clipper ship, it guess it was a day or two.† Of course, she was worried all the time.

Paul Stillwell: Was there any attempt, then, after you were ashore on Ford Island, to get the *Utah* people back together again?

John Vaessen: No. No attempt at that. They were all split up. I understand 110 of them went to the *Detroit*. I remember when they had a draft, and Warris, they asked him, because he kind of run things. He needed six electricians on the *Honolulu*, so he said, "Gee, I've got seven rated." So he said, "You better take them all. They all know each other."

"Well, we only need six."

---

* The official ship's history of the *Argonne* reports that a .50-caliber bullet from the direction of Ford Island went through the ship's port side. It killed Seaman Second Class Pallas F. Brown and killed Seaman First Class Leonard A. Price, both of whom were from the *Utah*.
† Pan American World Airways had a long, close association with the U.S. Navy. Before World War II Pan Am developed service facilities on a number of islands that served as way stations for Clippers, the flying boats that flew to the Western Pacific.

He said, "You're going to take seven." They went.

Paul Stillwell: How much contact did you have with him afterward?

John Vaessen: Oh, after, we had quite a bit of contact.

Paul Stillwell: Did he set up some place where *Utah* men reported in?

John Vaessen: Yes, it was an unfinished barracks. They were building new barracks on the officers' golf course, and they were a wooden building. The windows weren't in. Of course, out there it didn't make much difference. There was no running water. We all went out to a hose bib out in the yard that the guys put the hose on to mix the cement and so forth. That's all there was. That's where we washed up and everything else. He did get us mosquito netting and a bunk. He called us all around. Isquith is my chief engineer, and he wouldn't let me go. He says, "You're in no shape to go out anywhere. You're going to stick around here. We're got a salvage job. We've got to get all these ships up and going again."

Paul Stillwell: Why didn't he think you were in shape to go?

John Vaessen: I was black and blue. I was in a hell of a shape. I was integrated.

So anyway, Warris called us all around, those that was left, those who hadn't been assigned to other things, and he says, "I've got a brother over in town. I can get some money from him. I'll get about $5.00 apiece so you can get supplies, toothpaste, razors, things you're going to need. Of course, I'm your CO, I expect to be paid back," because it's against regulations to loan money. So he says, "I know you'll pay me back when you get paid."

So that afternoon, he called us over and says, "It won't be necessary, because Congress or somebody has passed a thing, and all you do is put your name and put 'sailor's mail' over in the return address," and there was no postage required. This was the main thing. Then we were all given—I've forgotten where the stuff came from—a toothbrush and toothpaste and a razor. I think I've still got the razor. It was one of these old Gillettes.

Paul Stillwell: A safety razor.

John Vaessen: Yes. It's all turned green.

Paul Stillwell: Were you ever compensated for the personal effects you lost in the ship?

John Vaessen: Yes, I was—75 cents.

Paul Stillwell: Total?

John Vaessen: Total! And as big as a Sears catalog attached to it, all the papers. I had to go through all these people's signatures. You know, I can't lay a hand on that damn thing. They had a list of all your personal effects. I had a wristwatch, and they said it wasn't authorized. I had postage stamps, stationery, a comb, razor, that stuff. Seventy-five cents.

Paul Stillwell: You had uniforms too.

John Vaessen: You were given a credit on that, but there were no uniforms to be had.

Paul Stillwell: Did you eventually have to buy replacement uniforms?

John Vaessen: Yes, a long time after before I could get any. You couldn't get any because they didn't have them. We were given a credit, I think, of $100.00, something like that. But it took me over a year to get clothes because nobody had it. Price was going up all the time.

Paul Stillwell: What did you wear in the meantime?

John Vaessen: Out of the lucky bag. I went downtown and had a pair made, whites.

Paul Stillwell: Did they have any way of tracking what your pay record had been?

John Vaessen: I don't know. They got the records, because even my record, when I got transferred once, there's a photocopy. It's about that big. I don't know how they do this.

Paul Stillwell: I wouldn't think they would have sent your pay record to Washington, though.

John Vaessen: Well, I don't know. We got paid. It wasn't that much to worry about.

Paul Stillwell: You didn't have any back pay due?

John Vaessen: Everybody had money on the books. I had money in my locker.

Paul Stillwell: And that also was lost?

John Vaessen: It's still there. Because when working on salvage, these divers had come, had worked for Merritt, Chapman & Scott in New York, a salvage outfit. I don't know if it's still in business. Anyway, they were all sworn into the Navy. They were going to go to the Red Sea. The Italian Fleet was scuttled out there at the time. All of a sudden, they said, "We've got a bigger job, more important, at Pearl." So they were shipped over to Pearl to do that job, and I got to know some of the divers pretty well. They went down in the ship, went through the hole I came out, and I told them where my locker was, the best I could—they had charts and everything—and where the E division headquarters was. They said, "Gee, that's about 15 foot of mud. We just can't get to it." But they did get the laundry, got the money out of there and a few other places.

Paul Stillwell: But you had no way of proving how much money you had from the books?

John Vaessen: No. We figured we were going to be going to the States and we'd need that money. We had the cash. My friend John Wallis, he liked to play dominoes, dice. He said, "Here I've got $40.00." And his sister had sent him civilian clothes to wear in town so he wouldn't be stuck out like a sore thumb, like the rest of the people. He put them in his locker, and he said, "I'm going to put it right in between my clothes." It's still there. They had just arrived the day before.

Paul Stillwell: Getting back to Warris, you mentioned before the tape started that he was a former enlisted man who had tattoos on his arm.

John Vaessen: Yes, all up his arms.

Paul Stillwell: Maybe his enlisted experience led him to being sympathetic to your concerns at that point.

John Vaessen: Yes. I must say he was fine.

Paul Stillwell: Did you ever have any contact with Captain Steele after the ship sank?

John Vaessen: I never had seen that man, never in all my life. I just heard stories about him, that's all.

Paul Stillwell: How long did this temporary arrangement last in the makeshift barracks with no water?

John Vaessen: I guess about a month.

Paul Stillwell: What did you do for head facilities?

John Vaessen: We went over to the receiving station. It was built for 200, and they had a regular master-at-arms there that would let you in. You didn't dilly-dally. You went in there. You ought to see the chow line they had there; it was continuous. People would get in line and say, "What are they serving? Is this breakfast? Is this lunch?" [Laughter] Just continuous.

I saw one sad experience in the chow line. They gave each guy an orange. A shipment had come in. There was one guy that would take it and he'd roll it in his arm and hit it, and make it bounce. He let it roll up his arm and go like this. Here comes the yard workman comes running up there, and he sees the guy doing that. He begged him, he said, "Please, are you going to eat that orange?"

He says, "Oh, I don't know."

He says, "Could I have it? I have a diabetic child at home and I can't get this kind of stuff." So the guy gave it to him. Those are the kind of little things.

Paul Stillwell: What other little details like that?

John Vaessen: I have to think. I can't do it all at one sitting, that's for sure.

Paul Stillwell: Were you working on this salvage project during the time you were living in that barracks?

John Vaessen: We had been assigned to it. We hadn't started. How did we do that? I think we started there, and there was four of us—Wallis, myself, Truett Davis, and Gunderland, and Charlie Tides, he drove Captain Warris around. There was five of us. We were each given a truck, and Charlie Tides was given a car. The trucks were destined for the Philippines, I guess, because the speedometers on them were in metric. They were Dodges, I think.

Paul Stillwell: What were your actual duties on the salvage work?

John Vaessen: As these guys were sworn into the Navy, they were all divers and professional salvage people.

Paul Stillwell: You're talking about the Merritt, Chapman and company.

John Vaessen: Yes. They were formally. They were Navy people now.

Paul Stillwell: What was the purpose for that?

John Vaessen: Because they knew what they were doing.

Paul Stillwell: Why put them in the Navy, rather than just hire them commercially?

John Vaessen: To get on a naval base, you've got to be sworn and all this kind of secret stuff. Nobody wanted to know what was going on, I guess.

Paul Stillwell: So you were used mainly as a truck driver?

John Vaessen: We did other things. We would get them acetylene bottles, get nitrogen and oxygen, and anything they needed. They were going out of their mind, the way the Navy operates. This Lieutenant Walker, the redhead, he wanted to get some buckets one day, and they said, "You'll have to get a requisition and you'll have to go up to the ad building and get some guy to sign it." I think he ended up in the ding-dong factory.

He says, "For chrissake, they want to get this job done or not?" [Laughter] You know, all this. We knew the routine by this time. You get this guy to sign it and this guy okays it, and all that kind of stuff. So anyhow, we'd take them to the warehouse where the stuff was kept in, and they'd ride with us.

Paul Stillwell: By knowing the system, you could be a real help to them.

John Vaessen: A lot of help. Oh, yes, they were all good guys. In fact, one of them wanted to go to the officers' club and get a drink. He was a hard-drinking guy. Andoll was his name. So he goes over there. He'd dive down, I mean, he'd do anything, none of this picky-picky stuff. So his uniform didn't look the greatest. The brass on the hat was turning green. So he went there, and they threw him out. He was so goddamn mad! I never saw a guy get so mad. So he went down to the laundry room, where the guys put in the laundry to be done, picked out some clothes there, put them on, and walked in. [Laughter] He was still dirty, but they looked better than what he had.

Paul Stillwell: Do you remember any of the specific ships that this group was working on while you were involved in salvage? Certainly the *Utah*.

John Vaessen: The *Utah*, no.

Paul Stillwell: They at least went ahead, looking for these—

John Vaessen: This was later on. First of all, the *Nevada* was the highest priority. The *Tennessee*, I think. They wanted to get it out. It was trapped. The *California* they let settle. The Pacific Bridge Company was doing a big job out there, and they had the pumps and everything put on there to pump it, because it was sinking pretty badly. They let it settle in five days because they couldn't risk civilians aboard the ship. This was backward thinking. But they were willing. So that's what happened to the *California*. Of course, that ruined everything. The salvage, the first thing they did is get a small arm and the ammunition that was still there, like off the *California*, the *West Virginia*. On the *Arizona*, they dove for ammunition on it. On this truck we would bring it up to Lualualai.

Paul Stillwell: That was the ammunition depot.

John Vaessen: They would rework it so it could be used again or something. We liked to do that because the Hawaiian territorial guard, they had one of them at every bridge you went over—little bridge, big. They would stand there and weren't quite sure what we were, and they'd give us a big salute. [Laughter]

Paul Stillwell: Sounds like a very makeshift existence that you were living.

John Vaessen: Well, we subsisted on the *Rigel*, and that was good food on that.[*] They had a cooks' school on there. The *Rigel*, did you ever hear about that ship? The superstructure was wood.

Paul Stillwell: I didn't know that.

John Vaessen: That was a kick. But we got so we'd eat around. We'd try all. We'd go to the sub base, because they had a school over there, and we'd find out what was there. After you know your way around.

Paul Stillwell: Did liberty resume after the attack?

---

[*] USS *Rigel* (AD-13) was a destroyer tender.

John Vaessen: Not right away. Around Christmas, I think it did. It was daytime liberty. We could go in the morning, I think from 9:00 to 5:00 or something like that, and then you had to be back. When the sun went down, you'd better be back.

Paul Stillwell: Were there rumors still rampant after a while, or did they gradually calm down?

John Vaessen: Well, they kind of calmed down, but there was more and more people coming all the time from all different places. I'll never forget the first ship, a transport, to arrive after the war started, was the *Harris*, and it had on it a Christmas tree, bicycles, Christmas ornaments, all that kind of stuff. All the stevedores took all that stuff and just threw it in a heap. You know what they shipped back?

Paul Stillwell: No.

John Vaessen: Dole pineapple. All the pineapple and juice, because they figured if they sent the ship back, they might not ever get a chance to get pineapple in the States again. They were going to have to get it out of there. It was all canned, ready to go. So that was good thinking there.

Paul Stillwell: They must have considered the island vulnerable.

John Vaessen: Well, yeah, we were all told what to do if taken prisoner, like I told you before. We didn't know. And the 55% Japanese population at that time. The women were turning their husbands in. They had sampans there for fishing boats, and they never had so many antennas.

Paul Stillwell: What do you mean, the women were turning their husbands in?

John Vaessen: They liked the American way of living. Japan was much different than it is today, of course. The man is supreme over there.

Paul Stillwell: How long did the salvage project last?

John Vaessen: I was there till June, and it went beyond that. I stayed until June of the following year.

Paul Stillwell: June of '42. You probably remember the *Nevada*, then, going into dry dock.

John Vaessen: Yes, that's where they give me the Navy Cross. Admiral Nimitz came on there.[*]

Paul Stillwell: I'd be interested in hearing your recollections of that event.

John Vaessen: I had no idea what they were talking about. Commander Isquith come out to me, and he says, "I'm going to want you to take your whites and send them to the laundry so they're good and clean." Up in Aiea, there was a laundry up there.

"You know, what's this all about?"

So he says, "You got to go up and get the Navy Cross."

I says, "What?" So I asked around to get a *Bluejackets' Manual*.[†] I wanted to see what this was. So somebody had one, because the place where we were was formerly the—what do they call the radio shack on the base?

Paul Stillwell: Communications station?

---

[*] Admiral Chester W. Nimitz, USN, served as Commander in Chief Pacific Fleet.
[†] *The Bluejackets' Manual*, which has been published by the U.S. Naval Institute in various editions over the years, has long been considered the "bible" for Navy enlisted men. It is a basic textbook and reference volume on a wide variety of naval subjects.

John Vaessen: t looked like a long house to me, just a wooden thing. So they had taken that over. There was a *Bluejacket's Manual* in there, so we looked it up, Truett Davis and I. He says, "Oh, that's a pretty high decoration."

So, anyway, the stuff was sent up to the laundry. Commander Isquith says, "Tomorrow [or whatever the day was, in April] we're to go on the *Nevada*, and we've got to be all dressed up because the admiral's going to be there."

So we went on. We were all lined up by seniority.

Paul Stillwell: How many people altogether, would you say?

John Vaessen: I'd say maybe 20. The Pathe News was there, and they took movies of us. By seniority, I was down on the end, and there was a Marine beyond me. That was it. Admiral Nimitz hadn't been out there very long. He was pinning all these medals on different people, giving the speech and everything that goes with it. He gets to me, and they had a little dais with a little shelf on it, and the box was empty, used up. There was a captain over there. He says, "Get going. Open that thing up. Hurry up." It was surprising for me to see an officer ordered around like that. Anyway, he opened it up. He pinned one on me and then one on the Marine, and that's all they needed.

Paul Stillwell: Did Admiral Nimitz say anything to you specifically?

John Vaessen: Yes. He told me, he says, "With this you get $2.00 a month for the rest of your life." So I found out he was wrong. He didn't know. It's only as long as you're in the Navy. And I did get $2.00 a month.

Paul Stillwell: Where did that come from? Was it sent from Washington or as part of your pay?

John Vaessen: Part of your pay. It was just added in, $2.00 more than you would normally get.

Paul Stillwell: That must have been a very proud moment for you.

John Vaessen: Well, we came off the ship when the ceremonies was over. Like I said earlier, the ship was only painted on the one side, just what they were going to take pictures of.

Paul Stillwell: This is for the newsreel's benefit?

John Vaessen: I guess. Anyway, we walked down the gangway, and Isquith was right ahead of me. There was a Marine down there at the end, and boy, they give 'em a big, snappy salute, and he said, "Did you see that?"

    I says, "What's that?"

    He says, "A Marine's saluting you."

    I said, "No, that's for you. You're an officer."

    "No, it's for you. You go back up and walk down." [Laughter] So I did! And sure enough, it surprised me.

Paul Stillwell: Where was the *Nevada* at that point? Was she in dry dock?

John Vaessen: No, it wasn't in dry dock. They had some damage, but it wasn't that bad.

Paul Stillwell: She had been in dry dock, so maybe she was out by then.

John Vaessen: They were rushing the ships in and out, just get it done and get out of there.

Paul Stillwell: What was the basis for the Navy Cross, that you had stayed at that switchboard?

John Vaessen: It ties in with Commander Isquith. I'll tell you what it was. Being what I did, it gave him the idea to go over on the *Oklahoma* and have the yard workmen do all this work to see how many they could rescue there. But for me, for keeping the lights as long as possible, shortly after, one fellow came to me and says, "I swam to the top of the ladder because I could see the light." The light wasn't very bright, you know, it was going fast. But he said, "I could see where I was heading."

Paul Stillwell: That must make an impact on you, to know that perhaps he was saved because of your efforts.

John Vaessen: Probably.

Paul Stillwell: So that was in April, and you said you kept on until maybe June?

John Vaessen: June, yes. New construction. They were rushing everything then. A lot of stuff was being built, and things were under control out there then. They were hiring people from all over the country to come out and work, getting the ships in the dry dock. They were moving along in the salvage operation. Like the *Oglala*.*

Paul Stillwell: She had capsized at Ten-Ten Dock.

John Vaessen: I think it sunk.

---

* USS *Oglala* (CM-4), a minelayer, capsized during the attack on Pearl Harbor.

Paul Stillwell: She turned sideways.

John Vaessen: No, because the four of us took our trucks. We'd go to the receiving station every day and pick up a working party. Isquith had one rule: everybody sits on the truck and not your feet hanging over. You stayed with feet on the truck. We'd get about ten guys to each truck, and a bunch of sacks, and we'd go out to Barbers Point. We'd pick up sand. They would load it. We were driving the truck, you know, we were the big wheels by then. They'd stack it all on there. Then coming back, they had a seat to sit on with all this sand.

So we'd haul it back, and they'd take it on the *Oglala*. Under water, they would put it on the perimeter of the deck, and they kept doing this until it was built up, till it was out of the water. Then they started pumping it, and they pumped it all out. As it come up, they'd take the sacks over, and all of a sudden, a lot of them spilled, and down it went. So I don't know what happened after that. I was gone the second time.

Paul Stillwell: How did your living arrangements change after you were in that temporary barracks?

John Vaessen: They were evacuating all the dependent women, and the housing was right outside the base. So in one of the houses, we were the salvage crew right near the gate. We were assigned to this house. We had to keep the house inside up, and the outside, they had maintenance cut the grass, water the lawn and that. We didn't have to do any of that. But we had a pass to go in and out of the gate in our dungarees. Charlie Tides, I talked to him on the phone just recently, he said, "I still have the pass."

Paul Stillwell: So that was pretty comfortable living.

John Vaessen: That was nice. Of course, we had bunk beds in there, you know.

Paul Stillwell: What led you to leaving there after six months or so?

John Vaessen: They were building all these ships and they needed people for them. Little by little, they were taking people every day.

Paul Stillwell: Did you really have any say in the matter at all?

John Vaessen: No, absolutely none. You don't have any say in the Navy.

Paul Stillwell: I wouldn't agree with that statement, but I'm really focusing on your experience at that point.

John Vaessen: No, you don't have any say. It's new construction, and we need people there. I was in the nucleus crew.

Paul Stillwell: How did you get back to the States?

John Vaessen: On a transport. Was it Coast Guard? That was the *Arthur Middleton*, I think it was. The Coast Guard ran the transport.

Paul Stillwell: When did you reach the United States?

John Vaessen: It must have been in June or July, I don't know which.

Paul Stillwell: Where did you report in at that point?

John Vaessen: At Goat Island.

Paul Stillwell: Once again.

John Vaessen: Once again, Goat Island. They had bunks this time. They were wooden, but the wire bunks.

Paul Stillwell: Were you still a fireman first class?

John Vaessen: No, I was third class petty officer.

Paul Stillwell: When did you get rated?

John Vaessen: Nimitz rated me. Everybody moves up a notch. That's what he told me.

Paul Stillwell: The engineers, though, I thought, went directly from seamen first to second class petty officer.

John Vaessen: No, they go to third class, except your boatswain's mates are called coxswains. That's third class.

Paul Stillwell: So you did become a third class electrician.

John Vaessen: Yes, I was a third class electrician. Isquith saw to that. He said, "You've got a rating out of this, and you wanted to be an electrician."

I said, "Yes."

He said, "You were in the E Division." Of course, I didn't know him aboard ship. I never had met him.

This Ed Gurtz would make out an order, whatever we needed, like we needed sandpaper, for example, and he'd always put down one.

I said, "Gee, you've got to fill out a paper for one piece of sandpaper?"

"Oh," he says, "there's a reason for that." So he'd go up and get Isquith to sign it. He'd come back and then he'd make a four out of it. Always ways of getting around things.

Paul Stillwell: What you did reflected well on Isquith, so he was taking care of you.

John Vaessen: Yes. Yes, he was all right. A lot of people didn't care for him. I thought he was fine.

Paul Stillwell: Why did other people not care for him?

John Vaessen: Well, I don't know, really. Those who had dealings with him. I didn't have dealings with him until after.

Paul Stillwell: You came back to Goat Island. How long did you stay there?

John Vaessen: I was put on shore patrol for a while, because I was third class. We'd go over to Chinatown or one of these bars that were out of bounds, that kind of stuff.

Paul Stillwell: Did you get any specific training for that?

John Vaessen: No. You'd go to the police station and they'd say, "If there's a fight, you go in pairs. One of you go to the phone and call for help."

Paul Stillwell: Did you have any interesting incidents on shore patrol duty?

John Vaessen: Mostly drunks. If a place is out of bounds, that's where everybody wants to go.

Paul Stillwell: So how do you go about getting them out of there?

John Vaessen: You just tell them not to go in. Even foreign, British and all them, "Sorry, old chap," you know, and they wouldn't do it. There's other places to go. Then we'd go like down to the terminal, where the trains come in. They would keep somebody there. I didn't like that out of bounds because you have to stand out in front there. But I must say, every place I was ever stationed, the bartender would come in, say, "If you want to use the restroom or anything, come right ahead."

Paul Stillwell: What was the reason for these places being considered out of bounds?

John Vaessen: They were serving drinks after hours or under age or whatever the law was. I don't remember.

Paul Stillwell: Did you have cases of having to escort drunk people to the police station or back to a boat landing?

John Vaessen: No, I never had that problem. Some women come running up to us one night and said, "There's a fight." It was way up a flight of steps, so we just called the police. I mean, that's all you can do. I mean, I'm not going to go up there and get thrown down a set of steps.

Paul Stillwell: How long did that assignment last?

John Vaessen: I'd say maybe six weeks.

Paul Stillwell: So that would put it maybe getting on to late summer in 1942?

John Vaessen: Yes. Then I was assigned to the *Starling*, and I told you I went over and asked for leave. I got that. We got under way in '43 on that.

Paul Stillwell: When did the nucleus crew form up, late '42?

John Vaessen: There was some already there ahead of me. I mean, the yeomen and first class machinist, a couple of chiefs. I guess I was among the last of the nucleus crew.

Paul Stillwell: Where did you report to her?

John Vaessen: In Alameda, where it was being built.

Paul Stillwell: So you went to the shipyard?

John Vaessen: Yes.

Paul Stillwell: Where did you live while she was under construction?

John Vaessen: We got sent down to Treasure. When you're assigned to the ship, you're send down to Treasure Island, moved down here, right on the other side here.

Paul Stillwell: What were the living conditions? Were the wooden barracks?

John Vaessen: No, it was old exposition buildings from the fair. I never thought, when I went to the fair, that I'd be living in one of these buildings. They had put in showers and that kind of stuff.

Paul Stillwell: So they hadn't torn those down yet.

John Vaessen: No, they hadn't torn them down. They were still there. In fact, the one I was in was the railroad exhibit. I never thought I'd go back to see it. [Laughter]

Paul Stillwell: I bet you didn't.

John Vaessen: And that's where I told you the *Chandeleur* had the other half.* It was either converted or being built or whatever. I don't know.

Paul Stillwell: So did you commute daily from Treasure Island over to Alameda?

John Vaessen: No, we didn't go over there. We stayed right here.

Paul Stillwell: What sort of duty did you have on Treasure Island?

John Vaessen: I don't think there was too much of anything. They would muster everybody every day and roll call, and we'd get announcements. The skipper had us all come over to the theater and gave us a lecture of life aboard a minesweeper. He had been on a minesweeper before.

Paul Stillwell: Do you remember his name?

John Vaessen: E. D. Magether. He was great.

Paul Stillwell: Was there training associated with your time on Treasure Island?

John Vaessen: He sent us up to Mare Island. They were assembling some mines up there, and we got up there. I guess he read the calendar wrong, because they

---

* USS *Chandeleur* (AV-10) was a seaplane tender that was built in San Francisco under a Maritime Commission contract and transferred to the Navy on 19 November 1942.

had just finished by the time we got there. We were supposed to stay there and everything, so we came back. He said it would be a good idea if there was a boatswain's mate and myself were set up to see how these mines are put together at the ammunition depot up there. But he had the wrong date.

Paul Stillwell: Did you have any inkling on what the electrical plant was going to be like on the *Starling*?

John Vaessen: The day I went with the yeoman down there and took a look around, of course, there were hoses and everything around there. I could take a peek down, but you really couldn't go in there. They were either painting or welding or something. You don't get much of a chance to see anything like that.

Paul Stillwell: So for the most part, you were just marking time till the ship was ready?

John Vaessen: I think it was before it was in commission, I don't know when that was, maybe October or November, we moved aboard, but it wasn't the final ceremonial part. That was, I think, in the end of December.* I'm not sure. Anyway, we left New Year's Day, I know that.

Paul Stillwell: How were your living accommodations in the *Starling* compared with what you'd had in the *Utah*?

John Vaessen: Better. Rough-riding ship. God! You know, these ships were built for the British, and they turned them down because they were too sophisticated for minesweeping. They figured if you're going to lose a ship, you don't want to lose all this. We had the master and slave unit, all that kind of stuff.

---

* The *Starling* was commissioned 21 December 1942.

Paul Stillwell: What sort of hierarchy did you have in the E Division? Were you one of the leading petty officers?

John Vaessen: No, I wasn't the leading; I was one of them, yes.

Paul Stillwell: How many did you have in the division?

John Vaessen: I think there was about eight. My good friend on there was called Steve Young, and he was the darnedest guy. I mean, talk about wild! I liked him. He kept telling me that his father was going to be a senator, and I'd hear all these stories. Sure enough, later on he was a senator from Ohio.[*] Because one time we had to go down and get chest X-rays or something, and there was a rubber stamp, a P.I. in your record. I said, "What is that?" The son had been over to Spain with Franco's regime, and he says, "I was going to go to the Philippine Islands too."[†] But it turned out it wasn't; it was "political influence."

Paul Stillwell: I've heard those initials before.

John Vaessen: I used to go on liberty with him, and oh, gosh, have more fun, more laughs! We went to San Francisco, and we were coming back over to Treasure Island or Alameda, I've forgotten which, and gee, it was starting to rain. It was just pouring! So he takes off his shoes and ties the strings together, and puts them around his neck. We used to catch the train over there and get off up here, then take the bus down. I says, "Why are you wearing the shoes around your neck?"

He says, "These are my inspection shoes." [Laughter]

[End of interview]

---

[*] Stephen M. Young, a Democrat from Ohio, was then serving in the House of Representatives. He was in the Army during World War II, later elected to the U.S. Senate, where he served from 3 January 1959 to 3 January 1971.
[†] Francisco Franco was dictator of Spain from 1936 until his death in 1975.

Index to the Oral History of
Mr. John B. Vaessen, Pearl Harbor Survivor

Argonne, USS (AG-31)
Repair ship that was hit by U.S. gunfire at Pearl Harbor on the night of 7 December 1941, 83-84

Awards, Naval
In April 1942 Admiral Chester Nimitz presented the Navy Cross to Vaessen, 94-96

Barngrover, Chief Electrician's Mate John W., USN
Served in 1941 on board the target ship *Utah* (AG-16), 41-42

Bombs/Bombing
The target ship *Utah* (AG-16) was used for bombing practice in 1941, 45-47, 61

Boston, USS
Nineteen century protected cruiser that served as a receiving ship at Yerba Buena Island in the early 1940s, 19-20

California, USS (BB-44)
Battleship launched at the Mare Island Navy Yard in 1919, 17-18

Fulton, USS (AS-11)
Submarine tender built at the Mare Island Navy Yard in the early 1940s, 17-19

Hill, Chief Petty Officer William D., USN
While serving on board the light cruiser *Raleigh* (CL-7) at Pearl Harbor in 1941, aided in the rescue of Fireman Second Class John Vaessen from the target ship Utah (AG-16), 73-80

Isquith, Lieutenant Commander Solomon S., USN (USNA, 1920)
In 1941 served as chief engineer in the target ship *Utah* (AG-16), 74, 85, 94-95, 98-101

Leave and Liberty
In Southern California in 1941, 30-31
In Hawaii in 1941, 51-60, 63-65
In San Francisco in 1942, 101-102

Little, Lieutenant (junior grade) John G. III, USN (USNA, 1935)
Killed on board the target ship *Utah* (AG-16) at Pearl Harbor in 1941, 50-51

Los Angeles, California
Site of a large Naval Reserve training center in 1941, 23-27

Mare Island Navy Yard, Vallejo, California
    Activities in the yard around 1940-41 included new construction and refurbishing old ships, 14-19

McCandless, Captain Byron, USN (Ret.) (USNA, 1905)
    Commanded the destroyer base at San Diego, 1937-45, 28-33

Naval Reserve, U.S.
    Casual status for reservists in Northern California in the late 1930s-early 1940s, 12-13, 20-23
    Large reserve center at Chavez Ravine in Los Angeles in 1941, 23-27
    Reservists were not completely welcome when they reported in 1941 to the target ship *Utah* (AG-16), 41-42

Nimitz, Admiral Chester W., USN (USNA, 1905)
    In April 1942, as Commander in Chief Pacific Fleet, presented the Navy Cross to Vaessen, 94-96

***Oglala*, USS (CM-4)**
    Minelayer that capsized in the Japanese attack on Pearl Harbor in 1941, 97-98

Pearl Harbor, Hawaii, Naval Base
    Served as a homeport for the target ship *Utah* (AG-16) in late 1941, 48-70
    The target ship *Utah* (AG-16) capsized on 7 December 1941 as a result of being attacked by the Japanese, 50, 66-90

Peters, Chief Electrician John L., USN
    Served in 1941 as E Division officer on board the target ship *Utah* (AG-16), 41-43, 49-50, 71

***Raleigh*, USS (CL-7)**
    After being attacked at Pearl Harbor in December 1941, ship's personnel aided in the rescue of Fireman John Vaessen from the capsized target ship *Utah* (AG-16), 73-80

Salvage
    Work on U.S. warships damaged during the Japanese air raid of December 1941, 87-92

San Diego, California
    Make-work for sailors at the San Diego destroyer base in 1941, 27-34
    Liberty for sailors in 1941, 30-32

San Francisco, California
    Yerba Buena Island was the site of a naval receiving station in the early 1940s, 19-23
    Liberty and shore patrol in San Francisco in 1942, 101-102

Shore Patrol
 In San Francisco in 1942, 101-102

***Starling*, USS AM-64)**
 Minesweeper built at Alameda, California, and commissioned in December 1942, 21-22, 103-106

Steele, Commander James M., USN (USNA, 1916)
 Served as commanding officer of the target ship *Utah* (AG-16) in 1941, 62-63

***Utah*, USS (AG-16)**
 Famous criminal John Dillinger served in the crew in 1923, 38
 Steps toward Vaessen's service in the crew in 1941, 34-36
 Operations off the West Coast and in the Hawaii area in 1941, 36-40, 44-45
 Division messing and berthing arrangements on board ship in 1941, 39-40, 52
 Work of the electrical division in 1941, 41-50, 67-68, 71-72
 As a target for bombing practice in 1941, 45-47, 61
 In port at Pearl Harbor in 1941, 51-70
 Capsized on 7 December 1941 as a result of being torpedoed by the Japanese, 66-80
 Vaessen was rescued through the bottom of the hull on 7 December, 73-80
 Two *Utah* survivors were killed by U.S. gunfire at Pearl Harbor the night of 7 December, 83-84
 Work of salvage divers on the ship in the aftermath of the attack, 87-90

Vaessen, John B.
 Youth and early employment in California in the 1920s and 1930s, 1-14
 Served briefly in the Naval Reserve, circa 1938-41, 12-14, 20-30
 Worked at the Mare Island Navy Yard, 1940-41, as an electrician's helper, 14-19
 Stationed at the San Diego Destroyer Base in 1941, 27-34
 Service on board the target ship *Utah* (AG-16) in 1941, 35-80
 Rescued through the bottom of the hull of the *Utah* on 7 December, 73-80
 Activities at Pearl Harbor in the months after the Japanese attack, 80-99
 In April 1942 Admiral Chester Nimitz presented the Navy Cross to Vaessen, 94-96
 In 1942 did shore patrol duty in San Francisco, 101-102
 In late 1942 was in the commissioning crew of the minesweeper *Starling* (AM-64), 21-22, 103-106

Warris, Commander John F., USN
 Former enlisted man who served as executive officer of the target ship *Utah* (AG-16) in 1941, 61-62, 84-85, 88-90

Yerba Buena Island, San Francisco
 Site of a naval receiving station in the early 1940s, 19-23

www.ingramcontent.com/pod-product-compliance
Lightning Source LLC
Chambersburg PA
CBHW080611170426
43209CB00007B/1394